WHY NOT BE A MISSIONER?

WHY NOT BE A
MISSIONER?

*Young Maryknollers
Tell Their Stories*

Michael Leach
Susan Perry
editors

ORBIS BOOKS
Maryknoll, New York 10545

Founded in 1970, Orbis Books endeavors to publish works that enlighten the mind, nourish the spirit, and challenge the conscience. The publishing arm of the Maryknoll Fathers & Brothers, Orbis seeks to explore the global dimensions of the Christian faith and mission, to invite dialogue with diverse cultures and religious traditions, and to serve the cause of reconciliation and peace. The books published reflect the views of their authors and do not represent the official position of the Maryknoll Society. To learn more about Maryknoll and Orbis Books, please visit our website at www.maryknoll.org.

Published by Orbis Books, Maryknoll, NY 10545-0308
Manufactured in the United States of America

Cover photographs: (clockwise from upper left) Lisa Jo Looney by Sean Sprague, Father David Smith by Father Kevin Thomas, Sister Jocelyn Fenix by Sister Beverly Arao, Brother Michael Greyerbiehl by Sean Sprague.

Library of Congress Cataloging-in-Publication Data

Why not be a missioner? : young Maryknollers tell their stories /
    Michael Leach, Susan Perry, editors.
        p. cm.
    ISBN 1-57075-391-1 (pbk.)
    1. Catholic Foreign Mission Society of America—Biography. I. Leach, Michael, 1940- II. Perry, Susan.
    BV2300.C35 W49 2002
    266'.2'0922—dc21

                                                    2001007114

To the memory of
Brother Michael Greyerbiehl, M.M.

Contents

Preface

Joe Everson, once an attorney with a high-powered Manhattan law firm, rests on a large rock overlooking Lake Titicaca. He's just finished a hike up at an altitude of over 12,500 feet and is waiting to share Eucharist with his flock. When Joe's not serving as a priest in the Altiplano, he ministers to inmates in Peru's most notorious prison in Challapalca or to people with AIDS.

Margaret Lacson, a young Filipino with a feminist consciousness, empowers Japanese women who are victims of domestic violence. She finds strength in the community of Catholic Sisters in which she lives in Yokohama, and comfort in Zen meditation, which she practices near the sea.

Joe Bruener, a Maryknoll Brother and a former actor on the TV show *Taxi*, now rides a bike in Jilin City, China, where he teaches English to students at Bei Hua Normal University, witnessing the Gospel through his presence, and learning as much from his students as they from him.

Jim and Mags Petkiewicz moved as "twenty-something gringos" from Georgetown University to work with the poor in Oaxaca, Mexico. Parents of two healthy children, Mags teaches preventive healthcare to indigenous children and Jim helps local artisans earn dignified wages while working at home.

What do these five people, and sixteen others who tell their stories in this book, have in common?

They are in their twenties and thirties, and they are smashing the stereotype that today's young adults are self-centered materialistic slackers. They are, all of them, Maryknoll missioners.

The Maryknoll priests, Sisters, Brothers, and lay people whose stories you'll read here are not much interested in materialism but they are interested in sharing the Good News of the Reign of God with their brothers and sisters overseas. You'll see that they don't talk about their faith unless invited. They choose instead to try to *live* it.

The Maryknoll family of missioners has three branches: the Society of Fathers and Brothers, the Congregation of Sisters, and the Mission Association of the Faithful (lay men and women). All three entities share the same spirit and mission, but have unique features.

The Maryknoll Society, founded in 1911, is a community of priests and Brothers from the United States who choose to stand in solidarity with the poor and marginalized in Africa, Asia, and South America. They experience the Good News through establishing relationships of friendship with the peoples of the world as well as in liturgical life, prayer, and contemplation. They share this experience with others through sacrament, teaching, and example.

The Maryknoll Congregation, founded in 1912, is a religious community of women, mainly from the United States but from twenty-two other countries as well, who cross boundaries, whether cultural, social, religious, geographic, or economic to proclaim the Good News. Like the Fathers and Brothers, they serve in a variety of fields, including medicine, communications, education, agriculture, social services, and spiritual formation.

The Maryknoll Mission Association of the Faithful, founded in 1976, is a Catholic community of lay people, including families and children. Inspired by the Maryknoll Fathers, Brothers, and Sisters, they too participate in the mission of Jesus by serving the poor overseas. Their work includes healthcare, education, community-organizing, grassroots economic development, and the formation of faith communities.

All of the men and women who share their journeys in this book love living in different parts of the world and living in community. And they strive to love God with all their hearts and minds, to see the face of Christ in the poor, and to be the face of Christ to everyone everywhere.

Originally trained in liberal arts or education or law, they come from a variety of professions. All of them felt that something was missing in their lives, that God was calling them to something more. They felt drawn to service. They wanted to serve God and their neighbor. None of them expresses any regret about their choices and all of them look forward to continuing their mission work in exciting new places and in creative new ways.

So the next time you hear that young adults think only of themselves, please think twice. Or twenty-one times, the number of true stories in *Why Not Be a Missioner*!

Michael Leach and Susan Perry
Maryknoll, New York
January 2002

Introduction

As the stories in this book show, Maryknollers come in all shapes, sizes, races, ages, and political persuasions. Like the church. There are as many qualities as there are missioners, but most of us share certain characteristics:

Faith in Jesus and a spirituality of inclusion. Our faith in the Incarnate Word inspires us to leave our homeland to discover God in other countries, as did the Magi. We don't have all the answers, but we do have something unique to offer. We cross borders and break barriers in order to love and respect everyone, especially those abandoned or rejected by society. Letting them into our hearts and lives, we are changed, enriched, and, yes, sanctified.

A respect for other religions. Rooted in the Eucharist and traditional Catholic prayers, with special devotion to the Blessed Virgin, Maryknollers seek and celebrate the spirit and truth (John 4:23) in the customs, life styles, and beliefs of all people.

Openness to conversion. Maryknollers don't encourage a one-time change of religion as much as a lifelong process of turning the heart toward God—beginning with ourselves.

Love of justice. We stand in solidarity with people who are oppressed. In a world wounded by ethnic and racial violence, Maryknollers offer healing by celebrating diversity. Among people divided along religious lines, missioners promote understanding through dialogue. We defend the sanctity of every human life and raise our voice on behalf of the voiceless.

Generosity and hospitality. Stewards of God's gifts, Maryknollers share what we have and joyfully welcome friends and strangers alike.

Flexibility. For all our meetings and plans, the Holy Spirit often surprises us with a better course of action, one we hadn't expected.

A sense of humor. After we've left all to follow Christ and gone to the ends of the earth and prayed and discerned and did our best, only to discover it isn't good enough, it helps to be able to stand out in the pouring rain, hip-deep in mud . . . and laugh.

If this sounds like the life you'd like to lead, please visit www.maryknoll.org. We may have an umbrella with your name on it.

Father Joseph Veneroso

1 _____

Thank You, Gregory Peck, Wherever You Are

Father William Stanley

I've heard it said: "In the book that makes up each person's life, we have a God who writes straight with crooked lines." It is certainly true in my case.

Quite honestly, I cannot remember a time growing up when I thought of becoming a priest, not to mention a missionary priest working in rural Africa. In the suburban environment in which I was raised, priesthood was definitely not one of the career choices presented at our yearly Student Career Day. It was "something no one does anymore."

For as long as I can remember I had an interest in the law. When I entered college my focus was entirely pre-law; my goal was to get into a good law school, become part of the law review, and go to work for a top firm. I gained acceptance at my top two choices of law schools. Life was moving along on schedule.

Then God picked up the book that made up my life. It was rewrite time. . . . The truth is: I am here in Africa as a result of an inspiration from an old black and white movie.

Tired of studying one night, I felt like going out to a movie, but none of my classmates wanted to leave the dorm on a cold and snowy night. They preferred to stay inside and watch MTV or

HBO, but I wanted something different so I drove to the local art film house. I knew that they had a 9:30 show and I was ready to chance it—whatever film they were showing was what I wanted to see.

It was "Gregory Peck Week" and they had chosen six different films, one each day as a retrospective of his career. That evening they were playing *Keys to the Kingdom*. Peck played a priest who after a lifetime in mission was on the verge of being suspended. The local bishop had sent an investigator to look into charges brought by unhappy parishioners. The movie is a flashback of the priest's life as a missioner in pre-revolutionary China.

What impressed and moved me so much was the unvarnished portrayal of mission life—the difficulties as well as the joys, the cultural misunderstandings, the personal courage it took to be misunderstood and often unappreciated, the struggle of living in a community with fellow missioners, and finally the great satisfaction of seeing the community one has struggled to build up grow and prosper.

This is not to say that I decided to become a priest then and there. What I did receive from *Keys to the Kingdom* was a rare moment of clarity. I knew that I wanted more than what I had planned for myself. Rather than being so focused on self-fulfillment, I knew then and there that I wanted to give back, give of myself, work with and for others.

It was a conversion of sorts. There was no falling off a horse, no blinding light, no voice from above, but, all the same, the blinders fell off and I began to see new possibilities where I had seen none before. The very next week I stopped to read one of the hundreds of fliers that were plastered on the walls and billboards around campus.

I studied an invitation to find out more about the JVC, the Jesuit Volunteer Corps. My college was a Jesuit school and each year hundreds of grads participated in one- or two-year volunteer commitments throughout the United States. I decided to apply, not knowing what I would really do if they accepted me.

Bill Stanley greets an African friend after celebrating morning mass in Mugumu, Tanzania.

When the acceptance letter arrived and informed me that I had been accepted to go to Alaska, I had a big decision to make. I told my family and friends that this would only be a temporary detour from my plans. I received a deferment from law school and left for Alaska shortly after graduation.

The two years I spent on the treeless tundra between the Yukon and Kuskokwim Rivers in Bethel, Alaska, opened my heart and my mind to mission as a possible way of life. Living with the Upik Eskimo and Athabascan native peoples further expanded my horizons and helped me see things in new, creative, and previously unimagined ways. It was a struggle at times to find common ground with the young men and women I worked with in the group home and teen center in Bethel, but the struggle was valuable and helped to shape the direction of my life and the person I am today.

When I returned home after my mission experience, I found out how true the Jesuit Volunteer Corps's motto became in my life. I was indeed "Ruined for Life," as we liked to joke in Bethel. As one Maryknoller aptly put it, "You can't put the olives back in the jar once they are out."

I found that my family and friends, while very loving, could not understand that the temporary break had become a life choice. Since I had never mentioned any desire to become a priest, it was all a rather unwelcome surprise. I struggled to articulate my decision because I was not one hundred percent sure of what I wanted or what God wanted for me. The universal opinion seemed to be that if I "had" to become a priest, why not be one in the U.S.?

I knew that my vocation made sense only in the context of overseas mission and during that spring, I set out to look at the different communities.

My eventual choice was Maryknoll because its primary focus *was* mission and most of the society's personnel and resources were directed overseas. I was also attracted to the image Maryknoll presented of a Family in Mission—Brothers, Sisters, priests, lay singles, and families working together in the countries of the world. The many Maryknoll martyrs and their commitment to the poor also made a deep impression on me.

After seven years of formation (three of which were spent in Caracas, Venezuela) and nine years here in Africa, I can say that I am content with my choice. I've experienced many difficult moments and situations along the way but God has always surrounded me with caring and supportive individuals who have helped me get past the difficult times.

My ministry here in Africa has been directed to primary evangelization and serving the needs of the rural poor, mainly farmers. I have spent my energy trying to encourage and build up the local church. My aim is to work myself out of a job, to be the last foreign missioner in the area where I am working. My hope is that the next priest to take over will be a Tanzanian. My work is directed to that end, trying to make the mission self-supporting in personnel and resources.

I came to Tanzania with fixed ideas as to what a priest should be and what role a priest should play in the local church. Truth is, the people themselves have helped shape who I am and what I do as a priest. Many times they fashion roles for me that I do not totally embrace but I move with in order to share the gospel with them. For example, the area in which I live is highly agricultural and, as one of the recognized spiritual leaders of the community, I am expected to live a life that keeps me in communion and harmony with God. That way I can help to bring God's blessings to the people, especially in the form of rain. Only those living in a place where people actually live and die by the harvest can truly understand the central role that rain plays. So sometimes my job is to pray for rain, to ask for God's blessings on the land, the seeds, and the crops.

My role as a priest is also to be the comforter of those who suffer from illness, to ask for God's blessing on the sick, both the farmers and their animals. Often I am called to arbitrate disputes, to be the advocate for fair cotton prices, to be the safety-deposit box for the community's valuables. Another aspect of my priesthood is to mirror God's compassion and forgiveness to all those who have need of it, especially in the sacrament of reconciliation. In a culture where families all live in close contact with one another and where there are few secrets, people invite me into the most personal part of their lives and entrust me with their confidences.

I consider it a privilege to live and serve here in Africa; each day brings something different and unexpected. Some days being a priest means comforting a family who has lost a beloved child or parent; other days it means celebrating and dancing at a wedding, sharing in a feast.

Many of the things I am asked to do on a daily basis I have never been trained to do, nor would I have imagined myself capable of doing. I guess that is the beauty of letting go and trusting that God, the source of all things, is always present with us.

What I do as a missioner here reminds me of a story called *Stone Soup* that I read as a child. In the story a young man walks into a town in the middle of a civil war. Various armies have passed through and the people have suffered great hardships. The man goes to the town center and sits on a bench and waits. Slowly the townspeople come out from their hiding places to find out who this stranger is. The man takes the bag he is carrying and pulls from it a smooth gray stone. "I can make the best soup you have ever tasted from this stone," he claims.

Suspicious but curious, they supply him with a large pot, water, and firewood. He puts the stone in the pot and after a while tastes the soup and finds it wonderful. "If only I had some onions it would be beyond belief!" he says. So one of the people brings out a hidden cache of onions.

Slowly, in this manner, the stranger gets the people to bring out carrots, potatoes, beef, salt, cabbage—in short, all the ingredients they had hidden from the soldiers. Soon all the people are enjoying a magnificent feast that none of them would have even imagined possible. Out of fear they had hidden their gifts and only when they were brought together was real communion possible.

This is exactly what I try to do as a missioner here in Tanzania—to build up the local community with the many hidden gifts with which God has blessed each of them and all of them. It involves building up and encouraging the people's self-confidence and belief in themselves. Helping them to see themselves as loved and cherished by God and as people capable of taking charge of their lives and finding solutions for the many struggles of their lives.

Like the young man in the story, after the feast and after the people have begun to trust themselves, their gifts, and their neighbors, it comes time to take the smooth gray stone, put it in the bag, and move on to a new town. I believe that this is part of my work here as well, the ability to move on to a new place after a certain amount of time, to allow the people to shape the local church with their own hands and in their own way.

All in all, it has been a wonderful experience in mission and I look forward to the years to come. So, many thanks to you, Gregory Peck, wherever you are!

2

The Truth of the Resurrection in a World Turned Upside Down

Kathleen McNeely

The Gospel of Matthew tells the story of three wise kings who leave their own land to follow a star. They set out to find and honor the newborn King of the Jews. Their wisdom is tested when the star brings them to a poor child lying beside his mother in a stable. Logic would have told these men that their calculations were off, that they followed the wrong star and that their entire journey was folly. But their openness told them to accept this truth turned upside down. Although their image of king and messiah was challenged by what they saw, they trusted their hope and knew that they were exactly in the right place and they paid homage to the child they found.

These wise men tug at my heart because they were not afraid to leave their comfortable homes to follow their dreams. They were receptive to truths that went beyond logic. Their star-gazing took them to a different culture where their perception of the Holy was stretched to unbelievable limits as they bowed down to adore the king and messiah found in the face of a poor child.

As a missioner living among Central American people, I have come to know more deeply the ways in which my faith has asked me to turn logic upside down and to accept, in hope, the twists that life presents. In accepting these unexpected twists, I know that God is revealed and that I come to a much deeper understanding of the Christian faith, which, in fact, does ask us to forget logic and to trust in certain truths turned upside down. As a Christian I am asked to embrace the paradoxes of following a king born into poverty, recognizing strength in weakness, and believing in resurrection, which comes only after death.

I was not following a star when I first ventured away from my comfortable home. I was, however, following my heart's yearnings to be a part of a community of faith and to work for social justice. My parents, Rita and Jim McNeely, raised me with values that shaped these heart wishes. I am the third of six children and the first girl in the McNeely family. Growing up, my siblings and I attended Catholic grade school, and under the instruction of the Ursuline Sisters we learned the basics of our faith. When I moved on to a new high school and went through a terrible phase of wondering where I fit in, my mom reminded me to pray. She also took me to her charismatic prayer meetings where I felt a greater sense of self-esteem in the presence of a community of faith, love, and support.

My dad was a proud member of the Pipefitters' Local #120. During the nine years he served as president of the union, he worked on the construction site by day and convened union meetings one night a week. His co-workers often stopped by the house to discuss a recent strike or lay off or to talk about the state of affairs at the union hall. When my dad was on strike, we always knew why, and what had to happen for a settlement. We respected the farm workers' boycott and during strikes, we never ate iceberg lettuce or grapes, and we always "looked for the union label."

My dad was also a coach. No matter what sport any of us took up, he was our biggest fan. He would come to our games and give each of us pointers on how to improve. My dad taught us to play fairly and to recognize the value in being part of a team. When I think of my dad, I think of how he was meticulously weaving a strong thread of justice into the very fabric of my being.

My heart's desires found resonance when in college I was assigned to read a book called *A Black Theology of Liberation* by James H. Cone. According to Cone, one's faith and life in the community had to be intimately connected with the act of creating social justice. In fact, the only people in a state of grace were those who were transforming society into a more just place. I was immediately at home since this theology offered a way to unite my strongest heart wishes.

Cone's theology also brought discord into my life: this theology declared that God is black. My world flipped upside down. The images of God from the Ursuline Sisters' classes no longer worked. I had to stretch my understanding to firmly embrace a belief that God is always beyond the limits of my imagination. I read all the books I could find on liberation theology. I was especially delighted to learn that there were Catholics doing this same kind of theology in Latin America. I graduated from Denison University with a double major in religion and Spanish literature and then went on to get a master's degree at Harvard Divinity School.

My first long-term stint on Latin American soil was in the early 1980s. Shortly after graduating from divinity school, I joined Witness for Peace in Nicaragua. I thought the program was perfect for me. I would be immersed in a local base community practicing liberation theology and I would actively make a statement about the U.S. government's involvement in the war. When I first joined the team, I believed that my very presence would somehow protect innocent Nicaraguans from the evils of unjust policies formed in the United States.

The experience, however, turned my world upside down again. I did participate in base communities, but the Nicaraguans did not ask me to protect them. Not unlike Jesus' request of the disciples in the garden of Gethsemane, they just wanted me to wait

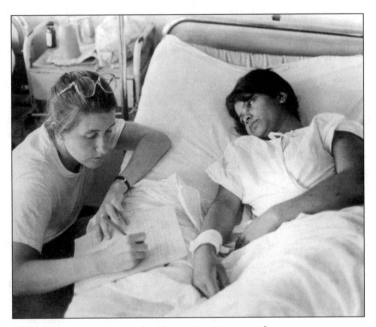

Kathy comforting a sick woman in Guatemala.

with them and to stay awake. The waiting part I figured out right away. I stood with Nicaraguans in the hot sun while we waited in bus lines. I waited with them for mail, for sugar, for diesel, for cooking oil, and for salt. I stood next to them at wakes, funerals, and hospital bedsides, waiting for their wounds of war to heal. The more I stood and waited, the more I understood the "staying awake" part. I had to be attentive to God's revelations—especially in the waiting. With a little attention I could see the face of God in the faces of people with whom I stood and waited.

In April of 1987, during a major contra offensive I traveled to several small settlements that had been destroyed. In the span of two weeks our small team went to a number of leveled villages to take photos of what remained and we visited morgues to see bodies and hospitals to interview survivors. I saw brokenness and weakness everywhere I turned. I was overwhelmed by the stories I heard and the broken bodies I saw. I wondered where God could be in all of this. When I returned to Managua to submit my affidavits, I remember getting out of the pickup and smelling the odor of decomposing flesh on my t-shirt. I felt like hope had left my side and that death had followed me to Managua.

Then, as I wrote my reports, I was amazed to find that even though death was overwhelmingly present, it never had the final word. Each time I conducted an interview to prepare an affidavit, I would read back to the person what she or he had said and then ask, "Is there anything you want to add?" In every case during two difficult weeks the person would add some remarkable expression of hope—a testimony of life in an environment reeking of death. I discovered strength, resilience, and hope in these people who appeared to be weak. This is where God was present—in the act of turning logic on its head and proclaiming life in the midst of death.

At that point, I would have made Nicaragua my home. However, I was in serious debt with student loans. In August of 1987 I returned to the United States to pay back my loans to Denison and Harvard. Three weeks after my year-long experience in Nicaragua,

I found myself in northern Massachusetts working as an associate chaplain at Williams College. The first few students who came to talk to me about their troubles were freshmen with roommate difficulties and complaints about noise in the library. I felt like I had set foot on a different planet. I wondered if I would ever connect with the students' world in any meaningful way after the intensity of Nicaragua.

A few months into the semester, a student was killed in a car accident. Visiting Cliff, a big, muscular football player who broke his leg in the same car accident, brought me to the realization that the brokenness I had seen in Nicaragua was everywhere and that I needed to "stay awake" and remain attentive to it. Cliff tearfully told me the story of the accident, the moment he realized his friend Charlie was dead and the journey by helicopter to the hospital where he lay. I sat with him, listened, and accompanied him as best I could. As I was leaving his room, a helicopter flew over the hospital. When I heard the sound of its propeller I was suddenly transported back to the hospital in Juigalpa, Nicaragua. I froze in my tracks in the busy hospital hallway.

I saw the face of Giselda lying helpless in a hospital bed much too big for her. Shrapnel in her abdomen from the attack on Kisilá ended her seven-month pregnancy. Then I saw the face of Lisette, a four-year-old in the children's ICU, crying out for water. I even began to smell the familiar stench of decomposing flesh. Fear crawled over me. Was hope once again taking its leave? Had death followed me to northern Massachusetts? I needed air. I quickened my pace and then broke into a sprint, running for the hospital exit. When I stepped into the cool, brisk autumn air, the sun was shining and I was surrounded by pine trees. It was these signs of life that told me that death was not the final word.

This flashback was an epiphany. I realized that while I had been able to recognize and stand close to brokenness in others, now I was being asked to be attentive to my own brokenness. My father, the person who had molded my passion for social justice, had died when I was twenty-one. The events around his death were a mystery. The coroner's report listed his death as suicide, but the circumstances caused us all to question it. Why would a left-handed man kill himself with his right hand? Why would a man who left notes everywhere and on all occasions not leave one then?

The unanswered questions lingered and so did my grief. I clung to the painful disappointment that my dad, my biggest fan, was no longer in my life. The most significant challenge of my life has been to overcome the impact of this event. While I had understood and appreciated how the Nicaraguans proclaimed life in the midst of death, seven years after the fact, I had not yet moved beyond my grief over my father's death. I had not yet been able to say anything hopeful. Just as the wise men twisted their expectations of the "king of the Jews" to fit the poor child they discovered, I was faced with twisting my grief and disappointment into belief that death is not the final word. I was challenged to make the theology of hope my own. I imagined myself going through a process similar to that of the people closest to Jesus. They felt so frightened and alone after his death that when the women went to tell them of the empty tomb they resisted; they wanted to cling to their grief. But once they embraced their own hope, the meaning of Jesus' life gave them the power to turn logic upside down and not only accept Jesus' resurrection, but proclaim it to the world.

I remember that spring in Williamstown. While I was walking down a road with a friend, I noticed every sign of life. All the trees and plants were green and in bloom; the colors were brilliant. Birds sang, ants crawled, and the sun warmed my face. I remember thanking God for how brilliant life becomes once one has touched death. Hope was becoming real for me and the more I embraced it, the more I was able to leave my grief behind. Still, I longed to return to Central America where I could be part of a community deeply sharing in this theology of hope.

After three years at Williams I paid off my loans and prepared once again to leave my comfortable home in search of more of God's epiphanies. Maryknoll was a logical choice, since in

Nicaragua I had met a number of Maryknollers who, like me, were committed to living in a community of faith while working for a more just society. After I completed the Maryknoll application, I went to work in Guatemala for several months as interim director at a language school in Quezaltenango. While the job was not a perfect fit, the setting was wonderful and I vowed to return to Guatemala. The following year I did, as a Maryknoll lay missioner.

The Guatemalans led me further into this theology than I had expected. The predicted lesson—that death is not the final word—was certainly a part of my experience, but more profoundly, the people with whom I lived and worked taught me what it means to embrace the resurrection.

I lived in Guatemala between 1992 and 1996. In those first few years the Guatemalans I came in contact with were afraid to take any leadership roles because repression and the threat of death had snatched away their self-esteem. Living in an environment dominated by death, they had lost their confidence in life. Daily I experienced the heavy, threatening presence of the military in the town where I lived. Through my work on the social pastoral committee for the vicariate I stayed connected to entire communities of people hiding in the shadows of the jungle.

But over those four and a half years in Guatemala, I also saw many signs of hope. The more people proclaimed these wondrous signs of life, the more things began to change. Exiles returned. People came out of hiding and insisted on being included in a new Guatemalan society that would recognize their human rights. People began to dig up bones and memories buried in the earth and in the hearts and minds of individuals who for years would not speak of their trauma and torture.

I worked in the Petén and traveled to small villages offering leadership training courses to women. While I worked in my own corner of the country identifying women leaders and watching their transformation as they recognized and celebrated their own self-worth, I witnessed that same transformation of people in the rest of Guatemala. A countrywide project begun by the Catholic Church called the Recovery of Historical Memory Project (REMHI) was a significant part of this process.

My office was housed in the vicariate's radio station, right next to the REMHI office. I remember the faces of the people, like Mateo, Antonio, and Chico, as they learned to use the tape recorders assigned to them, to conduct interviews, and to listen with respect to the stories of their fellow Guatemalans. They treated this as a sacred project, and were proud to be a part of it. I observed the transformation of these REMHI workers as they came to know themselves as worthy and loved by a God of compassion.

After three years of gathering testimonies, Monseñor Gerardi, the bishop who founded the REMHI project, gave the entire report back to the Guatemalan people in a celebration at the National Cathedral. I felt as if I was seeing a live version of Luke 13:10-14. When Jesus heals a woman who was bent over for eighteen years, she is free to stand up straight and tall and for the first time, she looks people straight in the eye. My companions stood straight and tall and beamed with pride that their project had come to completion and that the truth had been told.

Three days later, I was with other colleagues in the Petén when we heard of Monseñor Gerardi's murder. I was struck by the physical reaction of my friends. Their shoulders rounded, perhaps to protect their aching hearts; they slumped in their chairs and their eyes became fixed to the ground. An eerie silence took over. These same friends who just minutes before were chatting excitedly were suddenly speechless. This murder, so soon after a moment of exultation, threatened their newly found self-worth and dignity at its very core.

I joined busloads of people from all over the country carrying my candle and my red carnation at Monseñor Gerardi's wake. At the vigil Cirilo Santamaría, a missionary priest who worked closely with the REMHI project, asked everyone present to extinguish his or her candle. Only the Easter candle remained lit. We stood in the dark gazing at its weak light. We embraced the fear we felt when we heard of the bishop's death. Cirilo then asked two of the REMHI workers to come forward and to light their candles from the Easter candle; they then went out through the crowd lighting other candles.

It was more than symbolic to see a wave of light move through the crowd. As light infiltrated the dark night, hope returned to a people in despair. We let the light permeate our setting. Then, standing straight and tall, we proclaimed resurrection and light over death and darkness. Through Monseñor Gerardi and the REMHI project a number of Guatemalans now stood up straight and looked a culture of death straight in the eye. With dignity and strength they vowed to live the resurrection in an environment reeking of death and destruction. They chanted that Monseñor Gerardi was *presente* among them because his spirit and cause could never be killed.

Every day the Mayan-Q'eqchi' people of the Petén would greet me with their traditional greeting: *Ma sa' sa laach'ool* (Is your heart happy)? My heart was indeed happy to be a part of a community of faith involved in the work of social justice. I know that in following my heart I was led to this very place, to live in solidarity with a people learning to "stand up straight," to proclaim light in the darkness and to LIVE resurrection. Like the wise men, I was led to a place where logic would have told me I was in the wrong spot, but in touching the suffering of the Nicaraguans and Guatemalans, I recognized the face of God. I will forever cherish that gift for I now embrace a theology of hope through which I can accept the most illogical paradox of my faith: recognizing and embracing life and resurrection when death seems to linger around every corner.

3

A Mission Journey of Healing

Sister Euphrasia Nyaki

My given name is Euphrasia Nyaki, but I've always been called Efu. I am a Maryknoll missioner and you may be surprised to learn that I'm not American. I'm from Tanzania. I have been an "official" missioner for ten years, but it's hard for me to pinpoint exactly when my call to mission work began. In order to trace my call to this mission journey, I have to return to my childhood.

I was born in Tanzania in East Africa, in a small village located on the slopes of Mount Kilimanjaro. My tribe, known as the Chagga, is a very traditional and patriarchal tribe. Even when I was a child, I was very aware of the division of labor between men and women. I remember my brother being interested in cooking and being scolded by my father, who said that that was "women's work." Also, I noticed the basic inequality between men and women and that women were looked down upon and neglected. As a little girl, I listened to a lot of jokes that put women down or kept them in an inferior position. This seemed to be an ordinary part of our traditional culture, something that no one questioned.

When I was seven years old, I remember my father telling me that I was as stupid as my mother. Without hesitating, I replied, "No! If I am stupid, I would be as stupid as you, because I look like you." (People always commented on my strong resemblance to my father.) My father, who did not like that response or the tone of my voice, ran after me to punish me. As always, I escaped to the shelter of my grandmother's house. Even at that young age, I was aware of injustice and I was unable to keep quiet. The same is true of me today.

When I was thirteen, I was sent to a boarding school for secondary studies. This was my first long stay away from my family. The atmosphere at the school created another kind of awareness within me and I became a leader of the Young Christian Students Movement. The movement made use of the methodology of "see, judge, reflect, and act," part of the approach of Paulo Freire. We learned how to apply this methodology to our own situations, determined to defend the rights of students, workers, and teachers.

The Young Christian Students Movement stimulated me to question every motive of my actions. I also started questioning my identity as an African, a Tanzanian, a traditional woman, and a Christian. I began looking back to learn how my culture, customs, and rituals gave meaning to my life. I also questioned my Christian faith and its meaning for my life. At times I was very angry at the way in which Christianity was brought to us, dismissing and destroying our culture and customs in the process. These struggles within me continued for three years, until I finally asked myself if it was possible to continue being Christian and to maintain my culture and customs. In the end, I decided that when I looked at all that Jesus did and said, I found nothing at all that contradicted the teachings of my culture. I concluded that the problem had to be human weakness, especially on the part of those who brought Christianity to us. It was this process of reasoning, based in large part on the methodology of "see, judge, reflect, act," that led to my resolution to seek a way to integrate my cultural values and customs with my Christian faith.

I continued with the Young Christian Students Movement while I attended a teacher training college and actually became one of its national leaders in Tanzania. As a leader, I had the opportunity to meet people from many different cultures, which greatly broadened my vision. With this position of leadership, I was able to help other young people in their search for identity and to become grounded in their culture and faith.

Even before I had begun my college education, I had thought seriously about what I wanted to do with my life. I had decided that since I had gained so much clarity about my identity as a Tanzanian Christian woman, I should become a teacher so I could share my vision with others. After finishing college, I was invited by our local bishop to work at the diocesan Leadership Training Center. I enjoyed helping my students, especially outside of my regular classes where I taught physics and mathematics.

Three years later, several changes took place at the center and the bishop decided to convert it to a seminary. This decision was not welcomed by all because the training center had provided classes for both girls and boys, and the seminary would accommodate only boys. Eventually, the girls were transferred to secondary schools in the area. I felt it was unfortunate that the seminary's atmosphere and philosophy prevented us teachers from continuing many of the creative events we had planned for the students. I found this very sad, but it did give me pause to reflect and to create space for something else in my life.

My work shifted as I took on a new mission. On my own time, I started visiting women in the village where the center—now the seminary—was located. I learned their language and helped them form small groups where they had space to share their life stories. Their stories brought back my own memories of childhood in our patriarchal society and the tremendous need to promote equal rights for women. As African women, we talked and dreamed together of a just society where every person would be valued and respected.

I was happy working with these women's groups, but not completely satisfied because there still seemed to be something missing in my life. At this point, I was twenty-six years old; I had a boyfriend but did not want to get married. Of course, my grandmother and other members of my family worried that it was

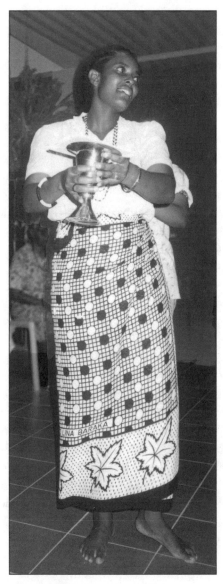

Efu in Brazil, dancing with the
chalice and paten, bringing Jesus,
Bread of Life, to the people.

getting too late for me to get married. Whenever I went home for family gatherings, I had to answer many questions about my life. In our African culture, particularly in Tanzania, being a single woman is not a viable option; it's neither understood nor accepted. A single woman is often thought of as a prostitute.

On the other hand, I was not happy living alone and felt a need for community. I started searching for a community of people with similar ideas who lived not just for themselves, but were committed to helping and caring for others in need of justice. It was hard to find such a place, because in Tanzania the only known communities were religious communities. I was not interested in religious life at that point because I was very critical of submissiveness and the role played by the hierarchy.

When I was ready to give up, I met a Filipino woman at the market. We struck up a conversation and I found her to be very friendly, free, and open. She invited me to her house, where I met two more women who were leading a workshop for a group of women right in their living room. I was very impressed with the relationship they seemed to have with the Tanzanian women. With no hesitation at all, I asked if I could work with them. I soon learned that they were Maryknoll Sisters. Working together we became good friends and eventually the Filipino Sister invited me to apply to Maryknoll. I hesitated because I thought of Maryknoll as a group of Americans. As I got to know them and learned that they were an international community with Sisters from a number of countries, I started the process of joining Maryknoll. I decided that although religious life was not something I had sought, living in a community might give me the support so I could approach religious life in a more positive way.

I went to New York for my three years of formation. After my early experience of culture shock in a land that has so much of everything, I found this period life-giving and transforming. It was hard for me to understand a vow of poverty in the United States. Why had I come from poor Tanzania to New York to take a vow of poverty? For these three years, I lived with eight other women of seven different nationalities. We learned so much about each other's countries and cultures as we shared stories of our people, prayers from our traditions, and food we prepared. Each one of us was challenged to bring the best of our culture to share with the others. We learned together how to understand and respect each other's culture and to adapt. This was not always easy for me. My culture, for example, truly values hospitality. We Africans thrive on having people constantly around us. I learned to understand that other cultures value privacy and that I had to give other people quiet time and private space.

During the formation process, Sister Grace, a member of a small cloister of Maryknoll Sisters, listened to my stories of growing up in Tanzania and helped me become aware of possibilities that lay ahead. She told me that my seven-year-old body had been marked by the suffering of Jesus and that this is what had brought me to an awareness of the need to fight for the rights of others who suffered.

As my spirituality was enriched by other spiritualities, my vision widened. I became convinced that the world is very small and that we are all one. I realized that wherever we go throughout the world we are going to find injustice and suffering. I had not been totally convinced of the value of doing mission work in a foreign country. Having done mission work in my own country, I knew that there was still so much to be done there. Yet from the moment I made my discovery about the smallness and oneness of the world, I was ready to go to another country to live with people from other cultures and to share my life and learn from them.

My first choice was Brazil because of its history of slavery and street children. Over one-half of the black people taken from Africa to the Americas were sent to Brazil. This seemed a wonderful opportunity for mission by an African Sister—the people and I shared the same roots. Also, I learned that the Maryknoll community in Brazil was composed of lay missioners, Brothers, priests, and Sisters. I was very attracted to this non-hierarchical community because I believe that different vocations complement one another and that we can learn from each other's ministries. It was, indeed, a very good choice for me; the sharing among the Sisters, lay missioners, Brothers, and priests has been life-giving and growth-producing.

It's been almost seven years now since I came to Brazil. These have been years of receiving and giving, with many pleasant surprises. When I arrived, I thought I would be working with street children in São Paulo and with basic Christian communities. Instead, I found myself developing other talents that I did not even know I had. The Brazilian culture of openness, friendliness, and generosity helped me discover and develop a ministry of healing. I began working with a Maryknoll team focused on women's health, rights, self-esteem, awareness, and education. We worked with Afro-Brazilian women whose self-esteem and identity had been terribly damaged by their situations.

I discovered these women had so many needs, especially health issues. Fortunately, I had my experience with the Young Christian Students Movement and with village women in Tanzania to draw upon. I began to explore and learn about alternative healing. While I had a very limited knowledge of herbal medicines in my own country, I was eager to learn and set about absorbing information wherever I could find it. My work with Afro-Brazilian women helped me to greatly expand my knowledge and to share it with them.

As I had hoped, the Afro-Brazilian culture did help me reconnect with my own roots of customs and rituals, which profoundly affected my spirituality. I recall vividly a conversation I had with a priestess from an Afro-Brazilian religion. We talked after a healing ritual that had lots of singing and dancing. All the people, including the children, were singing with so much confidence. I liked the songs, but I wasn't able to sing along with everyone else, so I asked the priestess if she had a tape of the songs that were used in the ritual.

She gave me a very strange look and asked, "Are you really an African?"

I said, "Yes! I am freshly from Africa."

She replied, "Your question surprises me because most of our customs are originally from Africa and I thought you would know them better than we here in Brazil who were separated from our roots." She continued, "We Afro-Brazilians pass on our traditions orally. We do not use machines to help us. You will learn the songs through your daily participation."

I was embarrassed and agreed with her that this was also true of us Africans. I remembered many stories told by my grandfather as we sat around a fire in the evening. I reflected on this and was very grateful that the Brazilian culture would bring me closer to my roots.

At times, the significance of my work nearly overwhelms me. The healing work I do with women, whether physical, emotional, or spiritual, touches my life so deeply; every time I connect with a woman in need is a moment of spiritual growth. I seem able to give life back to people, sometimes through a simple touch. My spirituality also grows because of the mystery of what I do. Whenever I participate in Afro-Brazilian rituals of healing, so many things happen that I don't understand and can't explain. I just have to accept and believe. As I reflect on this whole process, I feel I am beginning to understand what we mean by faith.

I am very happy that I had a call to mission as a young girl and that the call continued to pursue me. Every day I learn something new about myself and about others—about injustice and suffering and about how to help each other on our journeys. I understand now that mission is being in solidarity with one another and growing together in faith and that this process strengthens and deepens my own faith.

4

The Ambiguity of Brotherhood

Brother Michael Greyerbiehl

I am sitting in silence with forty other people participating in a contemplative retreat. With the summer heat and the sound of insects buzzing away like chainsaws, sweat slowly forms at the back of my neck and trickles down my spine. There is no escape and no relief, not in the super-heated breeze nor in the escape of fantasies of cold drinks and air conditioned rooms. My breathing becomes shallow.

When the bell rings, we all stand up and begin to do walking meditation. My back is completely drenched with sweat. As the odor of incense mixes with our forty sweaty bodies, the pungent smell is intensified by the heat. I'm concentrating only on the river that is running down my back. The beads of sweat cause me to shiver. The bell rings and we all bow and sit back down.

I'm studying Zen meditation in Japan, where I live as a Maryknoll Brother and work at a retreat house open to people of all faiths and spiritual backgrounds. It's very warm at the moment. I suffer from severe asthma and when I was ten years old in heat like this, I wheezed night and day and used to keep my brothers awake all night. Not being able to breathe is exhausting. Ultimately, that is what Jesus died from on the cross: he became exhausted from trying to hold himself up in order to breathe.

Childhood taught me much about the fragile shortness of life. A person with severe asthma is somewhat like a person drowning. The more they struggle to remain afloat, the more they sink. If someone comes to rescue them, the drowning person may pull the lifesaver under the water as well. The more I struggle to breathe, the further I get from breathing.

This weakness has given me a particular encounter and experience of God, the Spirit, and Jesus. And, surprisingly, it has also led me to the path of mission in foreign countries. Being able to live with a high degree of uncertainty and ambiguity and not just to survive but flourish has been a gift from God granted to me through my weakness.

Early in life, because of my asthma, I developed the habit of meditation and silent prayer. Sometimes just simply breathing itself was a prayer. Other times, one word wheezed in and out, such as "God" or "Abba." My long practice of meditation has turned into a special grace. Meditation has led me to Christian Buddhist encounters that have, in turn, led me to mission. My weakness of breath has also led me to study the Bible. I have always been attentive to the phrase "the breath of God," which has a key function in all the significant events of salvation history, beginning with the act of creation itself. It is this vibrant existence of God that grants life to all, refreshes the face of the earth, and renews the church.

Millions of people suffer with asthma in the world today. It is sometimes called the "poor person's disease" because the poor, who are more likely to be exposed to toxic environments and airborne pollution, are more likely to succumb to it. The poor are also the least likely to be able to afford proper medical treatment. I identify with them; it's a reality I cannot escape, no matter how hard I try. Together, in and through our weakness, we encounter our faith and discover the door of salvation. Missioners who live and work with the poor put themselves at risk and may even lose their lives in order to serve.

I was born in Saginaw, Michigan, in a family with seven children. I attribute a great part of my vocation to my family, who always inspired me to serve others. It was our family's response to a loving God. Though we were nine, there was always room for one more at the table. When I was about to graduate from high school I became interested in religious life. I was still searching for the answer to the question, What does God want of me? In 1982 I made my first contact with Maryknoll while I was at St. Louis University. There I met many priests, Brothers, Sisters, and lay people who shared their experiences of prayer and community life with me. I really felt like a missioner and, in fact, I was from that first day. I knew I would return to Maryknoll at some point.

I completed my degree in psychology at the University of Michigan and then did graduate work at San Francisco State University and the Adler School of Professional Psychology in Chicago. I worked in the field of mental health for ten years. Even with that experience, I knew I still wanted to choose the path of Maryknoll and service. I was also aware of a longing for prayer and community. After some sessions with a spiritual director, I was certain that it is God who calls and God who gives the gifts needed for living the vows and doing service. The deep mystery of this call stirred in my soul and penetrated my consciousness day and night.

Everything became effortless. I felt as if I had been searching for years through an endless maze for answers and suddenly the answer was right in front of me. During my time in the maze, I had often prayed with Thomas Merton, "My Lord God . . . I believe that the desire to please you does in fact please you. And I hope I have that desire in all that I am doing. . . but I have no idea where I am going." What had been unpredictable suddenly was known and it became both interesting and challenging. The experience of ministering to the needs of people—the sick, old, angry, hurt, hungry, imprisoned—from a faith center rather than a psychological model was radically new, energizing, and freeing.

Community was also something I had always longed for. Although I had experienced community to some degree with my friends, co-workers, and fellow students, a faith community was

Mike helping children with their homework.

another story. A community that prays together, lives together, shares meals together, and supports one another is balanced, integrated, and holy.

Working in the area of mental health had given me the opportunity to connect with the marginalized and poor. This connection stirred my sense of vocation as well. And I was attracted to Maryknoll because of its emphasis on work with the poor. It's ironic that I ended up being in mission to Japan, one of the wealthiest countries in the world. Making an option for the poor among the wealthy is a great challenge.

Knowing God's will for me has given me a sense of well-being that touches my physical, emotional, and spiritual life. God created me, designed me, and has called me to that place in which I can become holy and wholly my best. Little by little I move along this road. Ultimately, I have a "selfish" reason for joining Maryknoll's mission community: the life makes me happy and fulfills me.

It has been more than a year since I took my final oath as a Maryknoll Brother. It has been a year full of struggles and inspiration, challenges and opportunities, and awakenings and realizations of the meaning of being an invisible brother walking alongside Jesus in humble service. I have been challenged to forget myself and take up the cross of Christ. I am continually awed at how my weakness can become a strength and how my foolishness can become wisdom.

As a Brother, I often reflect on the story of Mary and Martha as I struggle for a balance between prayer and action. This story says something profound about the connection between Jesus' mission through both prayer and action. When I engage in "action mission," a joy-filled celebration of selfless service, I imagine Martha dancing in the kitchen, singing songs of praise as she prepares savory dishes for Jesus. When I am deeply involved in "prayer mission," I see Mary listening joyfully, deeply, compassionately to Jesus' stories of his journeys. I express my joy and gratitude to God, a joy and gratitude that transcend my own needs, as I pray, "Not my will, but yours be done."

It has been said that the vocation of religious Brothers is one of "the best kept secrets." Perhaps religious Brothers are simply trying to follow in the footsteps of Jesus by their quiet and occasionally hidden presence. Maryknoll's last Brothers' assembly proclaimed that "We have been touched by God to do the Will of God." If it were not for a sense of being touched by God, I could not be obedient.

While my faith journey has answered many questions in life, it has also opened windows of ambiguity. In his book *Blessed Ambiguity: Brothers in the Church*, John Paige writes:

> Brothers live "on the edge"; we tend to resent definition. We freely choose to eschew the facile grounded-ness of official function, status, or place in the church. By doing so, we keep company with prophets and live an intuitive experience that defies easy codification. Living this freeing, creative, prophetic experience of being a Brother renders our lives to more than one interpretation. Yet that is an ambiguity that we revere, a "blessed ambiguity," for it captures the reality of what we experience in the Church. (Landover, Md.: Christian Brothers Publications, 1993, p. 3)

Paige goes on to say that "Basically, all life is a mystery of grace and call." But what can be blessed about ambiguity? Similar words would be vagueness, uncertainty, doubt, indistinctness, haziness, dullness, lack of clarity—all with negative connotations. What is this "blessed ambiguity" that Brothers experience in the church? Does the ambiguity exist because the hierarchy of church has no place for Brothers? And the laity keeps asking, "What exactly is a Brother? When are you going to finish your training and become a priest?" Or does the ambiguity arise because Brothers can do just about anything, just like the laity? And then the laity wonders what the difference is, or if there is a difference.

Ambiguity is something that is being done away with today. From the breaking of the genetic code to the mapping of the heavens, humans appear to be racing further and further away from ambiguity in their lives. Has the fear of ambiguity pushed human-

ity to crave more and more clarity in all matters? Does this outer
clarity have a counterpart in increased inner clarity? Do people
have any deeper grasp today of their inner reality? But we must
remember that while technology and industry have "blessed" a
few with clarity, the majority of the world's people continue to live
on a subsistence level with daily ambiguity, including the fine line
between life and death.

The option for the poor taken by the Maryknoll Brothers roots
us in the humility needed to live out an ambiguous life style. It
takes courage to keep walking down the narrow path of Brotherhood with its many exits, roadblocks, and detours. Walking is not
done in blind faith or with empty hope. It is done in the knowledge that we are loved so deeply by God and that God's love
imbues all of creation.

In June of 1999 I was assigned to do preparatory work for the
Seventh World Assembly of the World Conference on Religion
and Peace (WCRP) at the United Nations in New York. The
WCRP is committed to the realization of each religious tradition's
potential for peace building and seeks to engage religious communities to cooperate on issues of shared moral concern. I was
part of a team of a dozen people working to organize the assembly. The atmosphere in the office at the United Nations was very
hectic and we were busy with correspondence from morning until
night. I worked closely with a Buddhist priest, who greatly influenced me. Both his personal and prayer life embodied a true spirituality of peacemaking and dialogue and a profound openness to
the ambiguity of everyday life.

We had many opportunities to exchange experiences of what it
means to be a Buddhist and what it means to be a Catholic and
what it means to be human. By sharing simple practices, such as
using the Catholic rosary and Buddhist prayer beads, we talked
about our beliefs and practices, what it means to be a peacemaker,
the nature of spirituality, and the meaning of suffering and death
in our different traditions. Together we searched and shared questions and answers to many mysteries in life.

During my time with the World Conference on Religion and Peace, I often reflected on the barriers to engaging in dialogue, a dialogue that could bring us closer to our humanity, to full brotherhood and sisterhood. The dialogue between my Buddhist co-workers and me revealed that both Christianity and Buddhism offer ways to experience death and to understand suffering. In the Christian experience, salvation is seen through death and resurrection. We have to die to ourselves with Christ and be reborn with him to new life. This paschal mystery is central to the evangelizing mission of the church.

Yet Vatican II made us aware that the paschal mystery is present not only in the church, but that it is also present among those to whom the gospel is preached—and is active even before missionaries arrive. The genius of the missionary enterprise is to convey this message in such a way that it touches the hearts and souls of those addressed.

In Asia today, the church strives to be a credible witness because people "put more trust in witnesses than in teachers, in experience than in teaching, and in life and action than in theories." People are "more persuaded by holiness of life than by intellectual argument." This was certainly true in the life of Mother Teresa. The Christian witness in Asia needs holy men and women who themselves are "on fire with the love of Christ and burning with zeal to make Christ known more widely, loving more deeply and following more closely" (John Paul II, *Ecclesia in Asia*).

All people, but especially we Maryknoll Brothers, are called to be such witnesses, people who participate in both contemplation and in action. Such brotherhood is my vocation—a road paved with service, mystery, ambiguity, risk, commitment, and closeness with God.

(On October 9, 2001, at age thirty-eight, Brother Michael Greyerbiehl died in Japan of a severe allergic reaction to an insect bite.)

5

Called to Mission

Patricia Curran

My name is Patty Curran and I have been called to mission. What that means is that I have been called to participate in restoring things to the way that God wants them to be. I kept stumbling onto ways in which we people have messed things up and even though I got pretty good at figuring out various ways of disassociating myself from all this, I see now that God kept right on calling and I spent a fair amount of time saying, "Could you call back later?"

Through phases of immaturity, self-absorption, and avoidance of anything painful, I tried to avoid the challenge of looking beyond my own circumstances. I grew up thinking that "global" meant runways in Paris and "mission" meant getting to be the most popular kid in my class. My plan was to live in Atherton, California, have a dark blue tiled swimming pool, and to learn to understand that part of the newspaper with all the little NASDAQ abbreviations and numbers. Honestly, if you had told me twenty years ago that I would spend the majority of my adult life in mission overseas, I'd have said you were nuts.

I grew up in San Francisco as number six in a family of ten surviving children with faithful parents who roused us from our beds to say the morning office and dragged us to prayer meetings on Sunday afternoons. My parents moved us to South Bend, Indiana,

34

when their charismatic community in San Francisco decided to merge with the People of Praise. While I resented anything that made me different from my peers in school, I later came to value that community as a place I went home to and a model of how to live in community.

I majored in social work at St. Mary's College basically because it was work that allowed me to be social. I knew "social" was crucial for me from the time in seventh grade when my Auntie Pat showed up at our house with the Myers Briggs test. Then one of my professors at St. Mary's proposed that I was at my best when I was interacting with others and that I could actually relate to people who did nothing for me strategically. "Apply it," she suggested. Work-wise, I graduated from answering the phones at a nursing home to being a member of the social services staff. It was a pleasure to visit with the residents and hear stories spill out from those who were ravenous for an audience. I learned then that listening is a true service. While working at the nursing home served as part of my foundation, my world was not rocked until I interned at the Department of Public Welfare. My job was to determine applicants' eligibility for Medicaid by visiting them in their homes. That was the first time things just simply did not add up. Suddenly things weren't tidy anymore and I could no longer separate myself from "those poor people."

I'll never forget one particular day when I visited an applicant at home. After the interview, as I walked down the stairs off her porch, she called out to me from the other side of the screen door to tell me that my shoes cost more than the money she had to spend on groceries for her three kids each month. There was no malice in her voice, it was just a passing comment. I remember thinking, "What the heck am I supposed to say to that, lady?" "Oh, really?" I replied with a nervous laugh, "OK, then, bye." Little does she know that she is partially responsible for my call to be in mission.

That was the summer before my senior year in college. At that time, my sister Kathy, serving with the Jesuit International Volun-

teers in Micronesia, was writing home of strange smells and won-
derfully odd experiences. She always seemed to be so happy in the
photos she sent us. After I graduated from college I volunteered
with the Sisters of the Holy Cross and spent a few months in their
Appalachia project, helping out at a community center. I guess
that was my "That Can't Possibly Be" stage. When people told me
how they had been conned by the mining companies to sell the
land below the top twelve inches of soil, I responded, "That can't
possibly be." And when they told me that, with no other options
available, they were forced to work for the very companies that
were destroying the land, my response was always the same. The
fog was being lifted and the bigger picture was becoming
startlingly clear. And with that clarity came a tension that has still
not been relieved. How is it that I have so many choices and that
being born into this particular body of mine has given me such
good fortune? And, harder still, as a Christian, what is expected of
me in the midst of it?

Then came my work in inner city Washington, D.C., where I
assisted the director of an emergency food bank and was a counselor at a grammar school. It was there that I was exposed for the
first time to AIDS and watched it suck the life out of a 26-year-old
mother. My responsibilities included things like taking a second-
grader to visit her mother who was in one of the local prisons. The
mother was incarcerated for manufacturing crack cocaine in their
basement. I also helped organize a children's celebration for black
history month and laughed until my stomach muscles ached during their Christmas pageant.

I enjoyed my work but separated myself from the reality of
those people's lives by socializing with my architect and lawyer
friends. Inner city by day and playing pool at the hippest spot in
town by night. Eight to five with the poor, and sailing, frisbee, and
Gauguin exhibits on the weekends. Life could not have been better. Then I found out, shortly before my volunteer term ended,
that I was pregnant. It felt like someone had shot a cannon
through my gut. But that feeling passed, due to the tremendous

KEVIN THOMAS

Patty Curran on mission in Cambodia.

support of my family, in particular, my mother. When I told her, her reaction was that that wasn't horrible news. Horrible news would be that I had lost my faith in God.

I progressed through the pregnancy confident that the best plan for the baby was adoption. That plan was fine and good until little Dillon was born. I spent plenty of time pleading that the best plan for me (keeping him) would seem like the best plan for him. Despite my efforts (ruling out one prospective couple because he was a tenor in the men's choir and another because she had a job that sounded boring), I found a couple who seemed deeply in love, full of faith, and committed to working for justice. Now, in the end, tucked away in my heart is the knowing that I can honestly say I made one unselfish decision in my life—I made the best plan for him. Simultaneously with giving Dillon up for adoption came a much deeper desire to serve and do something important with my life and become an instrument of God's love to others. Wherever you are, twelve-year-old boy, you served as my messenger.

As I was healing from the decision to place Dillon for adoption, I worked for a great couple outside of Washington, D.C. Their relationship served to confirm for me that I wanted him to have two parents. I have to mention Bill and Janet in this mission story because, had it not been for them and their witness as a couple, I think I would have lost my mind in regret over my decision. God provides on the darkest of nights.

Then I was accepted into the Jesuit International Volunteers myself (after all, I'm Kathy Curran's sister, a wild card that has come in handy my whole life) and was off to Kathmandu for the next two years. I worked in a Jesuit school and as a social worker at a recovery center for heroin addicts. It felt very, very good to be serving people in the name of Jesus Christ and living in community with people who challenged and inspired me. It was good to pray with the other volunteers, although it struck me as bizarre that our desire to live out our faith was sometimes the only thing we had in common.

When my term with the Jesuit Volunteers was up, I visited one of the Cambodian refugee camps on the Thai border and learned of the atrocities suffered by those who survived the war and genocide. There was a wedding in the village I visited and I was dumbfounded by how good they seemed to be at celebrating despite the horror in their lives. Months later, when a Maryknoll priest friend from my days in Nepal called and said that Maryknoll was sending lay people to Cambodia, I applied and was accepted. I must admit that a true servant would probably have been open to the invitation to go anywhere there was need, but I had my sights set on Cambodia. Had they offered me Tanzania, I honestly don't know if I would have agreed to go. There was something about seeing Cambodians dance in a circle and laugh.

And so I moved to Phnom Penh. After language studies and a time of discernment to consider where I best fit, I began working at Maryknoll's Wat Than Skills Training Program. Our effort was to teach skills to landmine and polio survivors whose disabilities prevented them from working in a traditional agrarian society.

I cannot count the number of stories people told of how landmines had destroyed their families by killing parents and children, by rendering their land worthless, and by making it impossible to live without fear that they and and their children would become victims of landmines, adding to the fifty thousand already maimed by the mines. Due to the nature of Maryknoll, which encourages missioners to spend time discerning where they best fit in, I participated in local peace efforts and worked with the International Campaign to Ban Landmines, two profoundly life-changing experiences.

In 1994, I participated in the Dhammayietra, a month-long peace walk of one thousand Buddhist monks, nuns, and lay people through the northwestern region of Cambodia. We were not aware that we were close to the front line and at one point we were caught in a cross-fire between government soldiers and a group of Khmer Rouge soldiers. A group of us foreigners was taken away, uncertain of our fate. Miraculously, as we walked through the jungle, we met up with a Khmer Rouge commander who let us go after he realized that our agenda was nothing more than accompanying Cambodians and spreading a message of peace.

After several hours of walking through one of the most heavily mined areas in the country, we found our way back to the other walkers. My sense of relief soon turned to revulsion and rage as several foreign journalists swarmed around me, eager to hear my story. It was startlingly clear that they had little interest in the families who were living in the midst of war due to lack of resources and options—their only interest was that I was an American.

Furthering my call to mission was the work with the International Campaign to Ban Landmines. Work at Wat Than provided me with ample information to share about the socio-economic impact of landmines. With adequate Khmer, I was able to translate for landmine survivors at several international conferences. I became aware at that point that I personally played a key role in bringing about social change. Prior to that, I had always felt a certain inadequacy in my work, almost as if I should be the one getting the coffee for the "pros" or that while I could be kind to people and helpful, it was not my responsibility to participate in changing structures. While those who know international law or work as surgeons are important contributors, so am I. And I think it would be a sin for me not to continue to believe this.

So the word "sin" has been redefined and, unfortunately, it no longer means taking the last cookies without permission or talking back to my parents. Sin is when God directs my vision and my experience toward how we humans have screwed things up and I look the other way or try to go about my business without confronting situations I know to be wrong. I'm ashamed to say that it is so terribly easy, particularly in this time of economic ease, for people like me to disassociate or distance ourselves from others' pain. This is what society's standards tell us to do, but it is sinful.

As a Catholic woman, I have to pray every day for that conviction so that I believe, deep down, that I must take responsibility

for bringing Christ's message of love to others. And that conviction is something I must relearn again and again. Just as Christ
took on the sin of the world without asking, "Is this my fault?" so
must I because I am a Christian. Mission is my awareness that I
can help make things right for *all* God's children. Because of my
faith, I am profoundly grateful for knowing that I am merely an
instrument for God to work through. The life of Jesus Christ, the
Son of God, must be the one by which I map my course and so far,
while it has been easy to get off course, he has waited patiently for
my inevitable return.

A fitting summary of my journey was a conversation with a
young friend, Nick, when I was living in Phnom Penh. Walking to
the market one morning we got on the subject of a fellow missioner. Nick said he admired her character, stating that what he
liked about her was how she didn't care how she looked or what
people were thinking about her. "She only cares about being nice,"
he surmised. "Sort of like me," I replied mostly (but not fully) in
jest. Nick had this look of utter conflict and consternation. After
what seemed like minutes of dead silence, he looked up at me and
replied, "No, Patty, you're not there yet." The "getting there" is my
mission.

6

Tae Kwon Do and Street Kids

Sister Chiyoung Pak

"Tae Kwon Do! Tae Kwon Do!" The shouts of eager students fill a church hall in Zimbabwe. This is a joyful moment for me in my work with the street children of Mbare, a section of Harare, the capital of Zimbabwe. I'm a religious Sister from Korea and teaching Korean martial arts is part of my ministry. Many people here find it hard to believe that I'm really a Sister from Korea and they are even more surprised when they find out that I'm a strict and demanding teacher. My students respect me, however, because they have seen martial arts on television or at the movies and they expect discipline and hard training. Sometimes I must laugh at myself: Tae Kwon Do is a form of self-defense, but these young people think they will have the skills of the movie stars!

When I look back at my life in Korea, my present location and work are even more surprising. I was born the youngest and the only daughter in a family of four children. I was a spoiled, selfish girl who could get anything she wanted in a secure world she controlled. Now I am in Zimbabwe, worrying and caring about the food, clothing, shelter, education, and health of children. I'm acting like a mother of children who are not part of any family! My sisterhood goes beyond my religious community because I have become the older sister of a large number of street children in Harare.

We never know where the journey of life will take us. It seems, though, that nothing happens simply by mistake; each event, both good and bad, in our lives forms the mysterious patchwork of who we are and what we are called to do. In the end, life, including the path we each take, is really a great mystery.

Although I became a Catholic when I was thirteen, I am still the only Catholic in my Buddhist family. I went to a Catholic church on my own to search for spiritual fulfillment, for faith. Becoming an "official" member of the church was not an easy task for me. After studying in preparation for baptism, I failed the first interview—and I was the only candidate to fail. I took the priest's question "Are you ready to be baptized?" very seriously and told him honestly and boldly that, "No, I am not ready." But I continued to study and learn more until I could respond with an equally honest and bold "Yes."

Even when I was young, I always dreamed of one world without any boundaries of language, color of skin, or different beliefs. My father traveled a great deal and I was strongly influenced by his stories of life in other countries. He encouraged me to have a wide vision of the world and told me of the value in reaching out to the world. So, here I am today, reaching out to the world in Africa, putting aside boundaries of language and skin color and belief, to share my journey.

Today, a typical day for me, finds me sitting on an overcrowded minibus. I am sitting beside Luckson, a sixteen-year-old boy who used to live on the streets. We can't even take deep breaths because all the passengers are pressed together. This is because buses don't leave until they can hold no more people; today we sat on the bus for forty minutes waiting for it to fill up. Zimbabwe has taught me patience, because sometimes even simple transactions take time, as does routine travel. I often joke with people that my name is not Chiyoung but Patient! It has been hard for me to learn to wait but now, after two years in Zimbabwe, I have reached the point where I can enjoy waiting without the feeling of suffering.

I have not minded the wait today because I have a lot on my

mind. Luckson and I are on our way to see Moses, a twelve-year-old friend of Luckson's. The boys used to live together on the streets. Moses is now staying with a woman who has four other children from a former husband. They live together in a shack that is so small that I wonder myself how they can all lay down to sleep at the same time. Moses's "foster" mother has no job and her current husband has left. With an unemployment rate of 70 percent, it's difficult to find work. Given these harsh conditions, she is focused on basic survival rather than giving attention to Moses. Without a mother's supervision, he seldom goes to school. Even though I provide support for his food and school fees and supplies, it doesn't seem to be working out the way I had hoped. This is why Luckson and I are going to see Moses, to spend some time with him, to encourage him to go to school regularly, and to let him know he has friends who care about him. We are also going to talk about Moses with his foster mother and the school's headmaster.

Missioners are supposed to write about their "success" stories, but I must regularly face my limitations and my challenges and realize that success does not come easily. Working with street children involves lots of pain and struggle. I need to support them very carefully and continuously in a way that doesn't undermine their own human dignity and pride. They ended up on the streets in the first place because of factors over which they had no control.

Tomorrow morning I will meet my small group of street children at a small swimming pool where they can have fun and play together, where they will be children for a short while. For them, though, the pool is not just a place to swim, it is also a place with a shower where they can wash their bodies and their clothing. They can find enjoyment in a positive way, without resorting to a more customary form of escape—sniffing glue. At night they are often too cold to sleep so they stay up all night sniffing glue and then sleep on the street in the daytime when it's warm.

For all of us the swimming pool has become a sacred place where we share our lives, our stories, and our hopes. Afterwards,

Street boys in Harare studying in the park with Chiyoung.

we go to the park for an hour where they study reading and mathematics with me. I always encourage them to go to school because life will be impossible for them without an education. After we finish studying, we spread a cloth on the ground and share a simple lunch of bread, peanut butter, and sometimes cheese. The boys each take turns serving the group. After the meal, before anyone leaves, they clean everything up and put the trash in the bin. In this way, they are learning to respect each other and the environment. When we are together, their happiness shows in their laughter.

Later, when some of the children decide to leave behind life on the streets, I want to help them find a home, a simple, two-room house where we can put mattresses on the floor for them, and provide support so they can go to school. I am happy to be working with this small group of children because each of them needs special care and the assurance of being loved.

Many of my Tae Kwon Do students are also street children and others are orphans living with their grandmothers who must struggle to support them and who have little control over them. I teach martial arts at the St. Charles Lwanga Learning Center, a school founded by the Jesuits in Mbare, a high-density, danger-filled area of the city that is an hour by bus from my home. Sometimes some of the boys from the street travel with me to protect me from pickpockets and other thieves. My two groups of students, young primary-school children and older secondary students, come from this poor, crime-ridden area. Along with Tae Kwon Do, I teach respect for each other and discipline, part of the special care that constantly affirms their human dignity. While appreciation isn't shown openly in their culture, their words, smiles, and greetings show me that they also care. Through Tae Kwon Do, we exchange our different cultures. I have hung a large flag of Zimbabwe in the gym. Each time we meet we greet each other in the Korean way by bowing and then we bow to the Zimbabwe national flag. Seeing the way we are learning to respect each other humbles me.

The spirituality that sustains my ministry in Harare as a Mary-knoll Sister and missioner is based on the unfailing presence of God. While the work is quite difficult at times, my spirituality is really quite simple and straightforward. God is everywhere. God is within my street children. When I look in their faces, I see God's loving face. When I look at their suffering from hunger, from cold, or from being without parents or family, I see the face of God in how they love and care for each other and in how they view life. They are precious to me and they allow me to see God every day—both in suffering and in happiness.

My life as a missioner in Harare, part of my journey beyond the boundaries, gives me great joy, whether I wait patiently for a bus, drill my students in their Tae Kwon Do "forms," or join in prayer for the people of Zimbabwe with my Maryknoll Sisters. I've never regretted that day when I was twenty-six years old and decided I wanted a more challenging life than I had working in an office. It was too easy, too comfortable. I wanted more. Today, my life of caring for the children of Harare who have no one else is more than I could have ever imagined.

7

Talking about God's Love Is Not Enough—I Must Show It

Father José Padín

My name is José Angel Padín Mercado. I was born in Anasco, Puerto Rico. I am the ninth child in a family of twelve, of which eleven are living and one is dead. My brother died when he was three months old. My parents named me after him. I consider him my guardian angel.

As I reflect upon my vocation I see that God's ways have not always been my ways. God has always been with me and has led me on paths that I never could have imagined. For a long time God knocked on my door and called my name, yet I kept on sending him to someone else's door.

But God's grace kept on breaking through.

The priesthood first attracted me when I was about twelve years old. At the time I kept it to myself since I didn't think that anyone else felt the same way, nor did I think I was good enough. I began to look into the diocesan priesthood but felt that this form of priesthood was not for me.

For a few years I kept hearing that "still small voice" calling me to the priesthood. At times I felt it strongly. Other times I forgot about it completely. I remember once saying, "Yes, Lord, you can count on me, I will be one of your priests!" Yet, there were other days that I got angry with God and said, "Why don't you try someone else, and leave me alone?"

God was patient with me and never gave up. He kept knocking and calling, knocking and calling. So one day I said, "Okay, I am going to try it just to prove to you that I don't have a vocation." Little did I know. . . . Once I tried it I couldn't see myself doing anything else, nor do I want to be doing anything else now.

Surely I had no idea that God would lead me to join a missionary group. I was drawn to the missionary life, its spirituality and work, through *Maryknoll* magazine (and since 1980 Maryknoll, *Revista*). Since my parents were, and still are, Maryknoll sponsors they received the magazine at home. I began to read it. The stories of missionaries in South America, Central America, Asia, and Africa inspired me. The magazine awakened my interest in mission, and my vocation became clear.

As a student I did my overseas training (mission experience) in Tanzania and Kenya. I worked for two and a half years in Africa before returning to the United States to finish my theological studies and get ordained. Since my ordination on June 14, 1997, I have been working in Mozambique, a new commitment for Maryknoll. This poverty-stricken country, with its good people, was left in ruins by two different wars: an independence war (1964-1974) followed by a civil war (1976-1992). The country is in poor shape structurally and economically, but even more so psychologically.

Mozambique is a country in construction and re-construction. During the colonial time the Portuguese oppressed the native people. The Africans didn't have the same rights, nor were they considered equals. Such treatment left emotional scars in the people's psyche; they suffered from feelings of inferiority and low self-esteem. Then came the two wars, which tore at the wounds and deepened them even more.

The people are in what I call "a cultural limbo." The civil war damaged traditional family values as well as social values; respect, responsibility, and honesty became out of fashion. Today, the youth do not have the traditional values that generally would guide them as they grow up. Consequently, there are many social problems: corruption, theft, prostitution, and so on.

As a pastoral counselor I have been working with youth in developing models and ways to process the cultural gaps. I try to help them understand their personal stories in the context of God. In this way they have been able to voice their experiences. The pain and the inhumanity of the wars are beyond words, but this process helps them to voice that pain and validate their experiences. Some of them have even told me, "I feel much lighter now. It is as if a great weight has been lifted from my shoulders." And others have said, "I never spoke to anyone about my feelings or fears inside me. . . . You are the first person to whom I have spoken about it. I feel good that I have done so."

As a Catholic missionary in Mozambique, I understand my mission to be a bridge of reconciliation—a link between the Mozambican and the Mozambican, the Mozambican and the white, and the Mozambican and God. Why? During colonial times the country was divided between the "*assimilados*" (those who absorbed the Portuguese culture, language, and values and rejected their own) and the "not *assimilados*" (those who did not reject their own culture, language, and values). This pitted the Mozambican against the white and, yet worse, Mozambicans against other Mozambicans. God was not part of the picture.

How did that happen? Whites were the "bosses and lords" then. They were the owners who controlled the resources for a decent living. They were the ones with access to schools and health services. They were the ones with good houses, cars, and stores. They were the ones who practiced the "white supremacy" of separation, creating a chasm between the Portuguese whites and the native peoples. When independence came in 1975, it brought with it the nationalization of everything, creating a feeling of payback-time for the Portuguese. Everything owned by whites was nationalized, including churches. Most of the whites had to abandon the coun-

José keeping company with some young men in Mozambique.

try in forty-eight hours, carrying nothing but a bag of clothing. At the same time, the government declared the death of God by saying that God did not exist. Anyone caught praying in any way was put in jail or beat up. This was directed at believers of all faiths, Christians and non-Christians alike. Brothers began to denounce their own brothers, sons were pitted against fathers, daughters against mothers, and family unity and values were destroyed.

I believe that people need to hear that God loves them, but even more do they need to feel it and know it. Wartime showed them the worst side of the human race. Even God-fearing people forgot about God. The socialist/communist government (1975-1994) said that there was no God. The war proved them right . . . at least so it seemed.

After all, where was God during the war? the people asked. Why did God allow so much evil and suffering to fall upon innocent and good people? These are questions young people and adults often ask me. The answers do not come easily. Words are easy to say, yet they can be meaningless unless accompanied by deeds. It is through good works (so do I believe) that God is manifested and God's presence is felt. It is through works of mercy and compassion, through examples of brotherhood and sisterhood that we can meet God face to face. As a missionary priest and pastoral counselor I am conscious that I should not be fixing people's problems. My task is to empower them to do their own healing. This is part of my mission.

Trust is essential for reconciliation. For the people here in Metangula, it is difficult to trust anyone, to believe that anybody can love them without wanting something in return. Thanks be to God, the people, especially the youth, are beginning to trust me, to know that I do what I do out of love, that I want nothing but their well-being. We are all children of the same Father that unites us.

I believe they have begun to trust me not only because I spend lots of time with them without asking for anything back, but because as a celibate priest I show my love for them. The sacrament of the priesthood is a sign of transcendent love. Priesthood is a choice made in order to better serve the people of God. It is a choice of life, not death, of love and service in the name of God. I think the people can see that.

To be a missioner is a challenge that one has to face every day. What does it mean to be a missionary? To me it means to be a witness and a voice of God's love, mercy, and compassion for all peoples. In other words it is never enough to speak about God's love; I must *show* God's love, God's mercy, and God's compassion in my day-to-day living. That is the most important part of my mission work. That is why I am a missioner.

8

Finding Myself in Japan

Sister Margaret Lacson

I did not set out to be a Maryknoll Sister or any other kind of nun. I always planned on having a family of my own. Yet, because an attraction to religious life made my heart restless, I eventually joined the Benedictines in the Philippines, the community I had grown up with throughout school and college. Their motto of *ora et labora* (prayer and work), coupled with my parents' religiosity at home, enflamed a desire in my heart to integrate prayer life into my daily life, but before the end of my novitiate, I left the community.

Eight days later, I found myself working with a Maryknoll Sister who was the executive secretary of an ecumenical organization of theologians from third-world countries, known as EATWOT. During the next five years, my world expanded and many of my views and beliefs were changed; others were also affirmed. I was immersed in the world of liberation theology—how the option for the poor calls us as Christians to live simply so that others may simply live and how we are called to change any societal structures that keep the majority of the world's population at the poverty level. At this same time, the women in the EATWOT organization were starting to articulate a theology from their own perspective. The discussions and activities in the office raised and deepened my awareness of women's issues.

Although this was a very satisfying and fulfilling time for me, something nagged at me. I still wanted more. I wanted to truly dedicate my life to work like this. While I could continue my work as a layperson, I wanted a community with which to pray and work. I wanted a group of people who shared my vision.

Gradually I increased my contact with the community of Maryknoll Sisters in the Philippines. Wary after my previous experience of what can be rigid structures within religious life, I saw that this community seemed more democratic and open to change. My "feminist" consciousness had taught me that patriarchal structures that allow one group to dominate another are usually unjust. I was looking for a community that encouraged participation in decision making, that enabled life, and that was respectful of human dignity and the integrity of creation. Hearing that the Maryknoll community in the Philippines had decided to do away with top-down leadership and had opted instead for governance by committees clinched it for me. Here was a group of committed women interested in the same things I was—the empowerment of women, the integrity of creation, and the changing of unjust structures.

When I joined Maryknoll in 1990, I spent three years in New York for orientation and preparation for mission. I was sent to Japan in 1993 and a new chapter opened in my life. With my background in liberation theology and my zeal for women's causes, it seemed puzzling at first to be sent to a first-world country where most women are still seemingly second-class citizens. Needless to say, Japan was not my first choice. Yet, trusting that God had reasons for sending me to Japan, I let it be, but kept my heart and goals clearly focused. Wherever I go, however I serve, my efforts will always be directed at empowering women, particularly poor women, at caring for the environment, and at changing mindsets to seek justice and equality.

My first years in Japan were filled with experiences of culture shock, but I had been told during orientation that I had to be patient while my body and spirit adjusted to life in Japan. Still, these were enriching years. I studied the Japanese language and Japanese culture. I also visited many temples and shrines in my attempt to understand Japanese religious traditions and the people's religiosity.

Knowing that real understandings of culture can come about only through working with people, I was eager for my first assignment at Micaela Ryo, a women's shelter run by the Rei Hai Kai (Sisters Adorers), a Japanese Catholic religious community. This put me in contact with women from Japan's lower economic levels. The women who came to Micaela often received financial support from the government's social welfare programs. Many were also victims of domestic violence and all were in need of empowerment.

During our meals together and as I cleaned rooms and refrigerators and babysat children while the mothers were learning new skills, I began to build relationships of friendship with them. As a listening ear and a supportive and caring presence, I tried to be part of their healing process. As they recovered physically from domestic abuse, they gained a feeling of security in this safe place and started to rebuild their lives. Given my resolve to work for the empowerment of women, this was fulfilling work and I could have stayed there forever.

But God had another plan for me. As a first-world country, Japan has drawn many migrants from poorer countries like the Philippines. For many years now, the Catholic Church in Japan has recognized the presence of the many migrants who fill half of their churches, with most from Latin America and the Philippines. After I made my final vows in 1999 and was reasonably comfortable with the language and culture of Japan, I was asked to work in the Filipino ministry program of the Catholic diocese of Yokohama, focusing on migrant solidarity and the training of parish workers. My work involved dealing with everything from unpaid wages, illegal dismissals, or accidents at job sites through Filipino women running away from Japanese husbands who abused them. Most of the Filipino women in Japan are undocumented and thus vulnerable to unfair labor practices. Those who

Margaret en route in Japan.

are documented and have Japanese husbands put up with their husbands' battering in order to safeguard their visas until they begin to fear for their lives or those of their children.

Listening to their stories humbles me: my problems are nothing compared to theirs. I am awed by the strength and courage they need to bear the problems of their daily lives. Life as a migrant in a restrictive culture and society like that of Japan is not easy and it is usually their faith in God or "Mama Mary" that helps them endure. When I feel their thirst for spiritual nourishment, I am challenged to dig deep into my own spirituality to find something to share with them that can help nourish them. In turn, they teach me to be strong in facing my own adversities.

The most unusual thing that has happened is the way in which my work with Filipino women is helping me rediscover my own Filipino identity. They are putting me in touch again with my own culture and the joy of my "Filipino-ness." After working hard to love and understand Japan, its people, and culture, being with Filipinos is a refreshing experience. Because I have learned to love and appreciate Japanese culture and religiosity, I am able to be a bridge—helping Filipinos understand Japanese and helping Japanese understand Filipinos. Coming from a solidly Catholic country, Filipinos have very little experience with other religions. I can help them see that God is also present in the Buddhist temples and Shinto shrines and to appreciate the other faces of God revealed in the religiosity of the Japanese society.

My circles of relationships continually feed my spirit. The community of Maryknoll Sisters gives me support, encouragement, and a sense of belonging while my Catholic parish helps me experience the uniqueness of the Catholic Church in Japan. The circle of Filipinos who bring their Filipino faith experience challenge me regularly to deepen my own faith. A warm circle of Japanese friends—neighbors, co-workers, and religious Sisters—teach me about the beauty of a people and their culture. Although I have left my family in the Phillipines, they are still very much part of me and their love from a distance warms my heart on lonely days.

Finally, one circle of people, a community of people who practice Zazen, has taught me new depths of faith.

I started practicing Zazen five years ago and now live with another Maryknoll Sister who is a Zen teacher. Zazen is an ancient form of sitting meditation in the Buddhist tradition. What can one gain from merely sitting? The power of Zazen increases as one enters more deeply into its practice. Even though I have only touched the tip of the iceberg of Zazen, I have already experienced the benefits in my life and my relationships. Zazen brings me back to the center, to the place of Deep Mystery within me. It has helped me become a better listener, to have peace in my heart, and to become a bringer of peace to others. It also helps me to better understand my own Christian faith and to become stronger in my convictions. It helps me to see the truth of what is real and it enables me to let go of what is not real or necessary. As I move toward a simplicity of attitude, I also seem to be moving toward a simplicity of lifestyle. The practice of Zazen, with its related art forms of the tea ceremony, flower arrangement, and Japanese calligraphy, requires a quiet heart. It brings me to a place where I can refresh and renew my spirit so I can respond better to the demands of ministry.

Quiet time spent with nature also refreshes my spirit. The sea is only twenty minutes away by bicycle and the surrounding hills provide great walking trails amid trees filled with birds calling back and forth. Yet, Japan is a land of stark contrasts. For me, the quiet of the landscape and the exquisite sophistication and beauty of the arts and culture jar startlingly with the stories of physical violence told by women abused by their husbands. Amid surroundings of such natural beauty, of ancient trees and clean river waters, how can these same minds that preserve and pass on traditions hurt other human beings or exploit the natural resources of other poorer countries? In Japan, as in the West, people can easily fall into the arms of materialism and consumerism. In my simple way, I hope that my life witnesses to a constant choosing for the heart of God, a constant turning toward what is good and pure.

9

Called to Life in Brazil

Angel Mortel and Chad Ribordy

One of the questions we're most frequently asked is "How did you come to a decision to serve abroad?" The answer, of course, is complex and even changes over time, as most stories do. However, there have been some constants.

Chad is originally from Wichita, Kansas. After graduating from Conception Seminary College with a B.A. in philosophy, he did a year of volunteer work as a youth minister with the Society of the Catholic Apostolate (the Pallottines), in an inner-city parish in Brooklyn. He then moved to Washington, D.C., where he worked for S.O.M.E (So Others Might Eat) at a homeless shelter for the mentally ill. During this time his desire to teach grew, and eventually he was offered a job as a religion teacher on the island of Guam, where he taught for four years at the Academy of Our Lady of Guam.

Angel, originally from San Francisco, studied English literature and third-world studies at Oberlin College in Ohio. After graduating, she also moved to Guam and was an English teacher working in the same school as Chad. Our relationship began there, on a tropical island in the middle of the Pacific Ocean. This was by far the most romantic part of the story! Two years later, we moved to Washington, D.C., where Angel began a master's program in international development at American University and Chad continued his teaching career at the Connelly School of the Holy Child, while earning his master's degree in pastoral theology through an extension program of St. Mary-of-the-Woods. After completing her master's degree, Angel went to work for Bread for the World, a grassroots advocacy group dealing with hunger issues.

And now for the more complex part of the story. Through our studies and experiences, we became aware of the inequalities in this world of "haves" and "have-nots." Our baptisms and our reading of the gospel message have challenged us to do what we can to bring the haves and have-nots closer together. Because of our backgrounds and the country in which we were born, we had always lived among the haves. During our time in Washington, we decided that we wanted to try to live a little more simply and a little closer to the have-nots.

After much discernment, we became a part of the Assisi Community located in an inner-city neighborhood in Washington. Learning about what it means to be in community with others was a truly wonderful experience for us. Those two years contained a great deal of laughter and tears. At the same time, although we lived among the have-nots, we were still somewhat isolated from them personally as we both had our busy jobs and our busy community life. We felt ready to pursue a dream we both had had even before we met on Guam—to be with the poor in another country, in another culture. But why another country, we are often asked. Isn't there enough to do in the United States? And the answer to that is the most complex or mysterious part of our story. We simply felt called. We believe that this is where God wants us. Somehow, through our family, our friends, and our studies, a seed was planted. And we decided that it was time to let that seedling grow.

We had always been interested in Maryknoll because we were long-time readers of the *Maryknoll* magazine, and we really liked the sort of things in which the missioners were involved. We also knew several Maryknollers, lay people who had very positive feelings about the group. So we applied. We were accepted, assigned to a country, went through an orientation program, and we now live in Brazil.

In the short three years we have been in Brazil, our many experiences of mission life have given us many topics for reflection: what it means to be a missioner from the United States, what it means to be a neighbor, what it means to be truly poor—these are just a few of the questions running through our heads while we are here.

Shortly after arriving in Brazil, Angel met a Brazilian priest who asked her where she was from. When she told him the United States, his mouth dropped open in disbelief. He told her that Chad, her husband who is tall, blond, and blue-eyed, was definitely from the United States, but he said she couldn't possibly be because of her brown skin and black hair. He insisted she must be Japanese or Chilean.

Angel continues to get this same reaction from other Brazilians. The dominant image of North Americans held by the average Brazilian is that they are white, tall, blond, and blue-eyed. While people are rarely surprised to hear that Chad is from the United States, Angel often must explain that, yes, she was born and raised in the U.S., that there are many brown- and black-skinned North Americans, and that ours is a racially and ethnically diverse country, very much like Brazil.

Another stereotype we often encounter is that all North Americans are rich. We've heard Brazilians say, "You don't have any money on you at the moment? But how can that be? You're American. All Americans have money." Or, "Can't you give a little more to the collection? After all, you're Americans." The idea that poverty exists in the U.S. is unbelievable. We recently met a man who asked us several questions about the U.S., including if there were homeless people. We told him that there are and, honestly surprised by this answer, he went on to ask: "How can there be

Chad, Angel, and their daughter Cecilia in São Paulo.

homeless people in such a rich country?" We told him that we often ask ourselves that same question.

There are also Brazilians who think we're crazy to want to live in Brazil. They can't believe that we would trade a comfortable life in the north for one of "poverty, unemployment, and violence" in Brazil. The thought is that everything must be better in the United States. Other Brazilians, upon hearing that we're Americans, avoid us—not out of dislike or hatred, but out of shame. They feel inferior to the rich American "experts" and see themselves as less because they are poor, brown or black, and uneducated. We've also met Brazilians who don't want anything to do with us because we are from the U.S. More than once, we've been in the midst of a group of Brazilians hissing at the mention of our country and Angel has actually hoped someone would mistake her for Japanese or Chilean. These Brazilians view the United States as the global oppressor—imperialists who bomb Iraq and deny food to Cuba.

This recent reaction from a handful of Brazilians has awakened a mixture of shame, anger, and confusion on our part. Our shame stems from being connected to a country that drops bombs on innocent Iraqi citizens; our anger, from being judged by the actions of our government instead of by who we are as human beings; and our confusion, from feeling lost in the question of what it means to be North American. How much of this North American identity do we want to openly assume, given the image Brazilians have of us? What needs to be challenged? What must we admit is true about this image? Our experience so far has made us much more conscious of our national identity and the responsibility, pain, and challenges that accompany that identity.

When we first arrived in our neighborhood, Jardim Guarani, we felt nervous about being in a strange and unknown place. Jardim Guarani lies on the northwest side of São Paulo. Most residents are migrants from the poor part of Brazil who have come to the city looking for work. Few can find regular jobs and the unemployment rate is over 55 percent. Our neighborhood used to be part of a forest reserve supposedly protected by the government, but few trees remain. The population has increased so quickly that houses practically sit on top of one another, clinging precariously to the denuded mountainsides.

We stopped the car in front of our newly rented house and started unloading our boxes and suitcases. Many of our neighbors sat in front of their houses chatting with one another, their eyes on our every move. They had to be wondering who these strange-looking people were. Knowing that we were being watched increased our nervousness tenfold. Just as Angel opened the car door to pull out a suitcase, she was startled by a little boy's voice saying "*oi*" (hi) behind her. She whipped around and was greeted by three smiling faces. When one boy asked if we were moving in, she said, "Yes." With a huge grin, he said, "Oh, so you're our new neighbors!" We introduced ourselves to Geraldo, Rodrigo, and Cristiano. We chatted a little and they went on their way. As they turned to go, Geraldo called out, "*Bem-vindo!*" (welcome). With the warmth in his voice and his words, our nervousness quickly disappeared.

Little did we know at the time that these kids would continue to touch our hearts. After that first day, our little neighbors, often barefoot and dirty, continued to come by to visit. They live with some other children in a tiny house two doors down. The front yard is filled with garbage and they have no running water or electricity. Someone told us that fifteen children and one adult live there. Basically, there are two families. Geraldo and Cristiano are cousins and Cristiano's mother takes care of all the kids in Geraldo's family. Geraldo's mother is in jail and his father wants nothing to do with the children. Apparently Geraldo's brothers and sisters are living with different aunts until their mother gets out of jail. Three of them live with Cristiano and his family.

The kids come by, chat a little, and then ask for something to eat. At first, we were taken aback. It hadn't occurred to us that such polite, joyful, and energetic kids might be hungry. We gave them each a piece of fruit. Soon they were coming by every day, sometimes three times a day, and five kids at a time. Neither of us knew what to do, so we continued to hand out food.

Late one night we were on our way home from downtown. We were at a bus station an hour's ride from our house. While standing in line to get on the bus, in the distance we saw a young boy, barefoot and dirty, begging from people waiting for their buses. We thought how sad it was that such a young boy was out that late at night begging. He couldn't have been more than eight years old. As he got closer, our bus line started moving. He ran toward the bus and shouted gleefully "Angelica!" Angel was startled to hear her name. In an instant she recognized Cristiano. She asked him what he was doing out so late, alone, and far from home. He said he was "working," that he had to bring home some change to help out his mother.

In all of our encounters with our little neighbors, we've felt sadness and joy and confusion. We feel sad when we see them barefoot, dirty, and hungry. We feel sad when the other neighbors on our street tell them to go away. But we feel great joy when we see them playing in the street, when they sing us songs, when they stop by to chat, when they ask how to say words in English. We feel God so present in them with their strength, perseverance, love, ability to survive, frailty, and innocence. It gives us great joy just to see them alive and smiling! At the same time, we can't disregard our confusion about how we should interact with them. Should we heed our other neighbors' warnings? Will they take advantage of us? Could we inadvertently get involved in something dangerous by being involved with these children? Or, should we put our total trust in God and "love our neighbor as we love ourselves," as we are called to do as Christians?

Although we still struggle with these questions, Jesus does give us an answer in the parable of the Good Samaritan. At the end of the parable, Jesus asks the lawyer, "In your opinion, which one of these three acted like a neighbor toward the man attacked by robbers?" The lawyer answered, "The one who was kind to him." Jesus replied, "You go, then, and do the same."

We have found that the poor often have profound reflections and interpretations of their own poverty. For example, this story was told by some children through a dramatic presentation for a Christmas Eve liturgy. The story began with a family from the northeast of Brazil, an area hard-hit by drought and unemployment. The husband, looking for a way to sustain his family, and the wife, very pregnant with their first child, fled their homeland and came south to the megacity of São Paulo. They ended up in a *favela* (shantytown) on the periphery of the city. The house was not much—a few boards slapped together, a dirt floor, no running water; but at least it was a roof over their head (leaky as it was), a place to call their own. But it didn't last long. The city decided that the houses in the *favela* were unfit for human habitation and would be torn down to build *cingapuras,* high-rise government housing. The family was forced to leave its small make-shift home just as the woman was ready to give birth. Having no relatives or friends in the city, they went door to door pleading for shelter but in the *favela*, every meter of space is already peopled. They finally resorted to sheltering themselves under the viaducts, where they were welcomed by some street children. It was there that a child, wrapped in swaddling clothes, was born unto the city of São Paulo.

The story was acted out in a small chapel in a *favela* near our house. The chapel is built into the side of a hill. Although visible from below, it is surrounded by houses and a maze of *vielas* (narrow passageways) and is hard to get to. Like so many buildings here, it is still under construction. People build when they have money and when the money runs out, construction halts. The rafters show, the outside of the church is unpainted, bags of cement mix are piled up inside the back of the church, and there is an assortment of used, creaky chairs to sit on.

We were deeply moved by the Christmas Eve celebration, especially by the children's dramatic presentation. These kids and their parents are poor, and the story they tell is really their story. Most people in the *favela* came from the poor northeast to the big city to find a job. Instead, they found more hardship, including sub-human housing and shelter. Like Mary and Joseph in Bethlehem, they were not welcomed and were often thrown from the little space that they could find. Nonetheless, there is a vibrancy in the community. The Christmas Eve celebration that night was not gloom and doom. The children smiled and laughed and the con-gregation of about forty sang with gusto as they danced and clapped their hands, accompanied by an out-of-tune guitar. Hugs and kisses were bountiful, candles and Christmas lights burned brightly, and bread and sweets were shared by all. This was a true affirmation of new life, new birth, new hope. As we walked home that night, we were grateful to celebrate Christmas Eve with them. Truly, Jesus was born again in our hearts through the lives of the people of this *favela*.

This is our life in Brazil. This is our life as Maryknoll mis-sioners.

10

From L.A. to China–
And Many Places in Between

Brother Joseph Bruener

Today is September 8, the feast of the birth of the Blessed Virgin Mary. I just returned from a massive celebration involving eight thousand people at the Lourdes Grotto in our diocese. And these eight thousand people are gathered together in China, not in the United States or Italy. I am currently stationed in Jilin City in China, not too far from some of the first Maryknoll missions in the area that was known as Manchuria. The mass was not unlike fiestas in Latin America, with throngs of people surrounding the grotto and food and souvenir venders everywhere.

I arrived a little late and was not sure where I belonged. When I asked one of the seminarians where I should go, he pointed up the hill where the bishop was standing and the priests and religious were assembling. It was a gloriously sunny day. I felt hundreds of eyes staring at me and saw mouths whispering "*wai guo ren*" (foreigner), as I pushed my way through the crowd and up the hill. As every missioner knows, despite a desire to take a back seat and only be a spectator, by nature of being different or from far away, we are often propped up in all kinds of places to beam like celebrities or angels. I am neither, but with this in mind I approached the rector of the seminary and asked, "Where do you want me?" He told me to process to the grotto behind the seminarians.

Just as I found my place, the procession started down the hill. The Sisters of the Holy Family led the way, followed by the choir, the seminarians, me (the only Brother in the diocese), the bishop, and the priests. It occurred to me that my place in the procession really reflected the nature of my vocation—somewhere between the priests and the seminarians. It is a vocation that is sometimes anonymous, but always a place of privilege.

What do I mean by "privilege"? Besides being grateful for my vocation, it seems to me that a Brother's life is free of many of the restraints that priests have; it also encourages the road to personal sanctification in ways that married couples often don't have time for or the resources to indulge in. And I use the word privilege because we religious Brothers are often invited to be in the "processions" and the front-row seats of people's lives. I'm equally pleased when someone treats me to a meal at a fancy restaurant or invites me for tea in an earthen-floor cottage. Such invitations show me that my "brotherhood" is special to them and so whatever they give is precious.

My vocational aspirations were awakened in third grade when Sister Bernardice asked one day how many boys in the class wanted to become priests. Many raised their hands, including me, though I knew even then that what I wanted was something different than the priesthood. I attended Catholic school in Wisconsin Rapids, a small city in Wisconsin. The Sisters of St. Francis of Penance and Charity who taught me during those twelve years were instrumental in my vocation. They always promoted the foreign missions, which resonated with my interest in other cultures. In high school, I was vice president of the Assumption High School mission club.

My home life was very stable and happy. I was the fourth of five children. As kids we fought a lot and played a lot, just like most everyone. The first eighteen years of my life were spent within a

Brother Joe praying with a Peruvian woman high in the Altiplano.

three-mile radius of home. Dad owned and operated our town's lumberyard in partnership with my uncle. By blood or marriage I was related to almost half of my grade-school class. We weren't poor, but I never realized until moving away how much and how little we had in central Wisconsin. Once described as the "Flatland Appalachia" by a New Deal politician, central Wisconsin offered an excellent though strict education, a taste for simple pleasures and people, and God played an important role in people's lives.

As a grade-school student I loved Lent. During Lent my family prayed the rosary together in the living room. We went to the Stations of the Cross on Fridays and we got a taste of life in other countries through the occasional UNICEF film that showed impoverished African children drinking bowls of milk. Along with dozens of other kids crammed into the school basement, I got a taste of what it might be like to serve in the missions. Although the reels kept breaking, the films gave faces to the babies we were saving pennies for during diocesan appeals.

Aside from the Stations and the occasional UNICEF film, I hated school. But I loved God and the Blessed Virgin. I grew up in an old-fashioned world and mine is an old-fashioned faith. It was the rosary, mass, and prayer time that started my vocation, and today those practices still sustain it. In Wisconsin Rapids at that time, a religious vocation was considered a "higher" call. I do strive to live out that call, but, honestly, cannot be as holy as people have a right to expect. (The first community I lived with called me Brother Patience, not for my strength of that virtue but solely because of my lack of it.)

After high school I attended the University of Wisconsin at Stevens Point and graduated with a degree in secondary education. I intended to teach English and drama. While in college I went to Guatemala for three weeks on a Maryknoll discernment program. This was a significant time that confirmed my idea of brotherhood and foreign mission work.

No one who goes to Guatemala can fail to be touched by the people. I wanted to help people in their difficulties and be part of their lives. We college students were exposed to the everyday life of the *campesinos*. We followed a seasoned missioner on his weekly rounds, including home visits, prayer groups, village masses, farm projects, and other programs. All fourteen students who took part in the discernment program returned to their own country with a profound respect for the Guatemalan people and for the Maryknollers. It was obvious that Maryknoll offered its members much flexibility—in living situations, finances, spiritual styles, ministries, mission sites, and so on. Maryknoll encourages individuals to develop according to their own talents *and* the inclinations of the Holy Spirit.

As eager as I was, I knew I had to finish my degree and gain some life experience before I could seriously investigate entering a religious community. Through the University of Wisconsin, I studied for a semester in both London and Krakow and then I completed twelve weeks of practice teaching in Kilkee, County Clare, in Ireland. In each place I was enamored with the people, their countries, and cultures, one strong indication of my "missionary disposition."

When I finished my studies, I drove to Los Angeles to try my hand at acting. I've always enjoyed performing. Although my parents were less than thrilled, I was determined and ready for adventure. I threw my clothes and $800 worth of traveler's checks in the car and took off. A friend from college who lived in the San Fernando Valley had invited me to stay with her for a few days until I could find a place of my own.

I was only twenty-three when I arrived in L.A. and it was the first time I had ever driven on a freeway. While I speeded along at 65 m.p.h., cars whizzed by me as I frantically prayed to the Blessed Virgin. Little did I know that in a very short time I would be driving among the fastest of the pack. My friend helped me find a room at the Alamo Hotel in North Hollywood. The cast of characters who lived there made auditioning for a sit-com wholly unnecessary: I found myself living on the set of my own show. However, the "Joe Bruener Show" didn't pay much, so I got work sorting clothes at the local St. Vincent de Paul store. I also sang telegrams, cleaned apartments, and taught CCD at St. Charles Borromeo Church.

Eventually a very kind talent agent took me on and six months later I landed a three-commercial contract with McDonald's. For the next year and a half I worked as a guest star on *Taxi* (a comedy series popular at the time) as a singing telegram deliverer, had a small part in a film called *Quirks,* and a few other odds and ends. In the end, though, I was desperately homesick and the continual lack of money made life seem precarious.

As much as I loved acting. I reasoned like the prodigal son, "Who of my father's employees does not live better than I?" I moved back to Wisconsin. It was the mid-1980s and there were few jobs to be had. Dad needed someone to help out, so I lived at home and saved my money for a year, intending to go to Paris to study French. When I announced my plans, my parents, once again, were concerned but resigned, and didn't argue about my decision, as long as I stayed out of debt and went to church on Sunday. They figured I needed to sort things out on my own and showed their basic faith in me.

I had been to Paris before and had also studied French for three years with minimal results. When I arrived in Paris this time I lived in a student hostel and later a roach-infested garret. I enrolled in a French language institute and after a year, to my great surprise, acquired a rudimentary conversational French, loads of wonderful memories, and more good friends. After I returned to Wisconsin, I continued studying French at the University of Wisconsin in Milwaukee and eventually passed the competency test to teach French in high school.

When I returned home there were still no jobs. Desperate for work, I moved in with an older brother and started working as a substitute teacher. I replaced teachers out on pregnancy or disability leaves. While teaching for three years and eventually getting my own English classes, I experienced both success and failure. It was at this point that I began to look at religious communities.

Looking back, I realize that I made a serious mistake by never going to the diocesan office of vocations. There are two distinct calls in religious life—the first is to the priesthood, sisterhood, or brotherhood, and the second is to a particular group. People in a diocesan vocation office are trained to help an individual sort out these questions. Although I had spent a lot of time praying about my vocation, I know now that I skipped an important step.

Working on my own, I chose the Christian Brothers (FSC). I learned a lot about community life that first year. The Brother who supervised formation drove home the point that what we do is never more important than who we are and that ultimately our mission is to help people cultivate a personal relationship with Jesus Christ. The year challenged me to grow in patience, generosity, humility, and more. When I began my ministry, I became the guest-master at a Christian Brothers retreat center near Stillwater, Minnesota. My responsibilities included scheduling retreat groups and coordinating their stays with meals, sleeping accommodations, and use of the facilities.

After a wonderful year, I decided that I did not look forward to teaching again and being in charge of disciplining a classroom, which would be a big part of my life were I to become a Christian Brother. The foreign missions continued to attract me, and it was with a hopeful and heavy heart that I applied to Maryknoll.

After being accepted, I moved to Maryknoll headquarters in New York to continue my preparation for brotherhood and to begin preparation for a mission overseas. The formation program for Brothers included a period of time doing ministry in the South Bronx. Working in a program for young children "at risk," I met a lot of dedicated individuals and two boys named Hector and William Garcia, who were nine and seven at the time. I started helping nine-year-old Hector with his homework and when I found out he hadn't been baptized, I asked his parents if I could take him to mass on Sundays. Hector's little brother tagged along. Eventually, both boys were baptized.

One winter morning I took them up to Maryknoll after mass to go sledding. I told them that Christians should always thank God for the good things in their lives and suggested that we thank God for the beautiful sunshine and snowy hill. As I bowed my head to listen to their prayers, William looked up into the sky from the top of our little hill and shouted, "Thank you, God!" as he shot down the hill on his cardboard sled. Since then, I have known and loved many people from various parishes, some even poorer than Hector and William, but none have been quite so dear to me.

After two years of mission preparation, Maryknoll's overseas training program (OTP) sent me to the Andean Region, which is made up of missions in Chile, Bolivia, and Peru. After a magical time at the Maryknoll language school in Cochabamba, Bolivia, I moved on to Curico, Chile. Everything had been so easy in Cochabamba, but before I could situate myself in Chile, I came down with a severe case of hepatitis A from some shellfish I had eaten. After three months of total bed rest I started to get better, but then was diagnosed with testicular cancer. After being in Chile only ten months, I was sent to New York for surgery. Radiation treatments followed and, understandably, my religious superiors were doubtful of my fitness for missionary brotherhood.

Eventually I was sent back to South America, this time to Peru, where I lived in a small town on the shores of Lake Titicaca with a Maryknoll priest and two Aymaran seminarians. The Altiplano is a place of fascinating customs, fiestas, and geography. I helped organize liturgies at two of the parish mission chapels and gloried in the gorgeous colonial churches, the crystal blue of Lake Titicaca, and the solitary shepherds chasing flocks of sheep and llamas across the austere landscape.

In the autumn of 1997 I returned to New York for my final year of formation. The Society continued to have reservations about allowing me to continue, but on May 30, 1998, I took my final oath to the Catholic Foreign Mission Society of America. The call to remain in religious life has always been challenging, and is perhaps even more so today. I have chosen to stay because I believe in my call from Jesus to be a Brother, as imperfect as I am. I believe in it even during the times when it isn't "fun"; neither did Jesus give up on his mission when he stopped getting a positive response. And there is nothing I want to do more. It reminds me of when Jesus asked Peter if he and the apostles were going to leave him like some of the less courageous disciples. Peter replied, "Lord, where would we go?"

My next assignment was China, where I am at present, teaching written and conversational English to students at Bei Hua Normal University in Jilin City. While my main job is to teach English, I am also involved in the lives of my students and the members of the parish where I go to mass on Saturday and Sunday. My patience, resolve, and dedication are being strengthened daily by my efforts to learn Chinese characters—without these three qualities, the task would be impossible. As I live my vocation in China, I am struck by the way in which it is enriched by the kindness of the Chinese people. The stories of the difficulties they faced during the Cultural Revolution amaze and inspire me to be a more dedicated Brother, to be more patient and attentive, to give more of myself, and to try harder to invoke the Holy Spirit at each turn.

I must continue to ask, "Where do you want me?" of the Holy Spirit. Whether I'm told to go to the rear, the anonymous middle, or the front of the procession, I accept happily, with confidence in my vocation of a missionary Brother, sure of my place in working to bring about God's reign.

_____

11

Legal Eagle–From Chicago to Nairobi

Christine Bodewes

At times, my vocation as a lay missioner with the Maryknoll Mission Association of the Faithful (MMAF) seems like an incredibly dramatic and unpredictable transformation and, yet, in the same breath it feels as familiar as sitting in my grandmother's old rocking chair. When I reflect back, I realize that the seeds for my interest in different lands and cultures were first planted by my father when I was a small girl. In every late night car ride of my childhood, I remember falling asleep to my dad's stories about his parents' flight from Eastern Europe to America. While my grandparents died before I could know them, the images of political and religious persecution in Europe intoned by my dad were very real to me. Over the years, these stories seeped into my heart and linked me to people who had suffered. I believe this lived history of my family instilled in me at an early age a deep desire to be active, not passive, in the struggle for justice.

However, my journey from a wide-eyed young girl infected with a longing to know far-off places to a Maryknoll lay missioner working in the slums of Nairobi took a somewhat circuitous route. After graduating from St. Mary's College at Notre Dame in 1987, I went to law school at the University of Illinois College of

Law. Immediately upon graduation, I traveled to East Africa for two months to look around and experience the people and culture of Kenya and Tanzania, places that had long been in my dreams. Upon arriving in Kenya, I instinctively knew that East Africa was my spiritual home. Deep down I felt that my heart was here first. Even though I subscribe to Ernest Hemingway's belief that if you are lucky enough to find your spiritual home, you should return there often, I did not anticipate ever going back to Africa.

Back in Chicago, I launched my legal career with a mid-size law firm of over one hundred lawyers called Sachnoff & Weaver. As a litigator (courtroom lawyer), I specialized in securities litigation. It was very challenging and extremely high-pressured work demanding up to eighty to ninety hours a week. Many of my clients were "Fortune 500" companies and the stakes were high, often with millions of dollars hanging in the balance in each lawsuit. And I loved it. After six years, I was made a partner at the age of thirty-two.

In addition to supporting a very sophisticated practice, the firm also encouraged a lot of pro bono work. As a result, I was able to spend about one-third of my time doing immigration and civil rights cases. I remember well representing a woman who had fled El Salvador. As a leader in her Catholic small Christian community, she had opposed the military government's persecutions and as a result was arrested, raped, and tortured. This woman, a gentle and quiet soul, opened my eyes to the remarkable acts of heroism that ordinary people undertake every day in response to the gospels.

During those years, I felt rooted in my faith as a Catholic and dabbled in all kinds of volunteer work, but that part of my life was only a shadow to my "real" life as a big city corporate lawyer. Although my career was going well, I had a nagging sense that I could do more—more for people in need, more for the world, more for God. I really struggled to learn how to integrate my faith and my work into my whole person. While finding my place in life remained elusive, I tried to fill the widening gap between what I was doing as a corporate lawyer and what I felt I wanted to do as a lawyer committed in faith, with more and more pro bono clients. But it wasn't enough.

A turning point came in 1996, when a very close friend of mine from St. Mary's College invited me to visit her in Cambodia. Several years before that, my friend Patty Curran had joined MMAF and served in Cambodia for five years. One day I watched Patty sitting in a circle of young Cambodian kids in a TB clinic, singing and clapping, and it struck me as such an intense witness to the goodness of God and life. While I didn't admit it at the time, I had a profound sense that God was calling me in the same direction. I was doubly lucky because another classmate and friend from St. Mary's, Heidi Cerneka, had joined MMAF. She serves in São Paulo, Brazil, and had also shared her mission experiences through many letters and stories. Both of these women influenced me greatly.

After my visit to Cambodia, I felt myself being more and more drawn to a life in mission. But I was scared to death. I was very nervous about making the life-style change. I thought I just couldn't do it. I had lived alone in my North Side apartment and enjoyed all the perks of an upwardly mobile career and income— travel, great restaurants, plays, bars, and the list goes on. The thought of giving that all up for a life of comparable poverty seemed too difficult. And my friends thought I was crazy. I also thought my legal skills would not be very useful in a mission context. I figured that I was a corporate lawyer, not a social worker or a doctor or someone who I believed would more typically have a role in a developing country.

And that is where the Holy Spirit comes in. For someone who has not experienced a "calling" (like myself up to that point), it can sound pretty hokey. I used to scoff at all talk of "vocation," but now I believe that God calls each of us in a special and specific way. For me it seemed clear that God was calling me to experience my faith and life with and through the poor. To this day, the "whys" of my calling are a mystery to me.

Notwithstanding my cold feet, I continued to feel called to

"Pro bono" work in the slums of Nairobi.

overseas mission. I started talking to both lay and religious people who served overseas in mission and, strangely, almost every person I met with pointed me to Maryknoll. So, two months after making partner, I called up the Maryknoll Mission Association of the Faithful and asked for an application. To my shock and great relief, I learned that they were looking for a lawyer to work in the slums of Nairobi. I knew right then that I had found my place.

My skepticism about whether I could transfer my corporate legal skills to the poor living in Nairobi's slums quickly abated upon my arrival in Kenya. To my surprise, the Maryknoll Fathers had a close relationship with a legal clinic called the Kituo cha Sheria in Kiswahili that offers free legal advice to people living in the slums.

To put it in perspective, over 55 percent of Nairobi's population lives in more than one hundred slums. These slum communities are located on less than 1.5 percent of the city's total residential land, making Nairobi one of the most densely populated slum cities in the world. These villages are comprised of one-room mud and tin shacks crammed together. There is no water, sanitation, lights, roads, or social amenities like schools and clinics. On top of the horrendous living conditions, people living in Nairobi's slums are terrorized by local police authorities and live in constant fear of eviction by the government.

While the Kituo lawyers give legal advice on virtually every topic, I focus primarily on the land issue, which is probably the single most important issue politically, economically, and socially in Kenya. In addition to filing lawsuits on behalf of communities who face unlawful evictions and demolitions, our team of lawyers helps these communities develop non-judicial strategies to stay on the land. We also do a lot of education in the slums around issues of land, housing, and human rights. In addition, we are researching and drafting alternative land tenure systems and land laws that we hope will be considered in the constitutional reform process.

My Kenyan colleagues are a small band of unbelievably committed people who are great lawyers and great fun. Advising people who are deeply mired in poverty and hopelessness is very challenging. In fact, it is a hundred times more difficult than my private practice was. Representing a community of hundreds or sometimes thousands of people can be overwhelming. In addition to the sheer numbers of people, the stakes are high. People stand to lose not only their homes and everything they have to their name, but even their lives.

In my first year here, my very first client, Joseph Kimani, was strangled and dumped in a mud puddle, all because he dared to tell the local authorities that as a Catholic he could not condone the unlawful land-grabbing in his village by the government. I will never forget walking into his family's one-room hut on Good Friday and listening to the wails of over a hundred women. In Nairobi I can't hide in a corner office on the thirtieth floor. My clients are right there with me in the slums and on the streets, not just in the courtroom.

My work here is also very different in another significant way. When I was practicing law in Chicago, I filed lawsuits to win, to get a favorable ruling for my client. Now, I never go to court expecting to win the case. The courts in Kenya, which are thoroughly corrupted, have never issued a ruling in favor of a slum dweller and against a title-holder. I file lawsuits to protect people's rights. I file a case because I believe people should not have to live in dehumanizing conditions and in fear that their home will be demolished or burned down in the middle of the night. The very act of filing a suit, which gives voice to my clients who are so accustomed to a shroud of silence, is a victory in itself. My Kenyan colleagues have taught me to redefine success and that has changed and liberated me. But I won't lie. Letting go of the desire and need "to win" is not easy.

I feel incredibly blessed and lucky for my vocation as a lay missioner with Maryknoll. It has allowed me to be of service to the poor and marginalized in a very life-giving way. And it has allowed me to know God in a very dynamic way. The people in the slums are mired in a degree of poverty that is difficult to describe. They have virtually nothing by means of material possessions. But even more devastating is that they have very little chance of ever improving their lives or the lives of their children. But over and over I am amazed at their unshakable belief that God is with them no matter how grim life seems. I have heard "*Mungu yupo*"—God is here—as people put their children to bed hungry, as they watch their houses burn down, and as they bury children who have died of AIDS. This kind of faith makes me feel that God is very close.

While Kenya is facing political and economic crises of disastrous proportions, hope is alive among the poor in Nairobi. And I have the privilege of witnessing and being part of it every day, which is the most satisfying work I could ever hope to do.

12

Caring for People–
Tanzania to Hawaii

Sister Bitrina Kirway

Who would have ever dreamed that a child of a simple farmer from the area of Arusha in northeastern Tanzania would be found one day in the middle of the Pacific Ocean, living and working among Filipinos, Koreans, Japanese, Caucasians, Chinese, Vietnamese, and Pacific Islanders? I certainly didn't, but God apparently did have a great plan for this child of God. Let me begin where I am now, in the middle of the Pacific Ocean, in Hawaii.

The part of Hawaii I live in is not shown in Hawaii's many tourist brochures. Most of the people who live on this side of the big island are low-income families that depend on government assistance for their basic needs. Sooner or later they will be cut off from welfare. In fact, the first cut came at the end of 2001. It's hard to know how this is going to impact these families. There are times when it's difficult to believe we are a part of the United States.

Since Hawaii has the highest rate of unemployment and underemployment of the fifty states, it is very difficult for people to find jobs, including individuals who have completed our training programs. I spend most of my time working with a program called Communities In Schools-Hawaii (CIS-HI), which is a project of the YMCA. The mission of CIS-HI is to strengthen families. It emphasizes traditional Hawaiian values, including genuine caring (*malama*), shared responsibility (*kuleana*), working cooperatively (*laulima*), loyalty to a shared mission (*kupa'a*), and living harmoniously (*lokahi*).

My primary ministry at CIS is to develop core skills that will lead to harmony in family life and employment. We use a system emphasizing family values (*ohana*) to help participants clarify what is important in their lives, to set goals for themselves, and then to develop readiness skills for employment.

Does this sound like the usual work of a missioner? Let me tell the story of one young mother who came to my life through the ministry that I am involved in. I'm going to call her Debra Nakamura, although that is not her real name.

Debra is an attractive twenty-seven-year-old woman who has a Hawaiian Japanese father and a Thai mother. (Many Hawaiians have mixed ancestry.) She came to my office one morning with her two lively children, Aulana (a four-year-old) and Justine (a two-year-old). Debra wanted to find a job. I told her that we didn't actually provide jobs but rather training that would prepare her to find a job and to keep it. She decided she wanted to try it out.

As I got to know her better, I found out that she was intelligent and determined to accomplish what she believed in. Her life was also much more complicated than one would have known. Not only was she an unemployed single mother of two small children, but they lived with her father, who lived with his girlfriend, who had a daughter who also lived with them, along with her boyfriend and two children! (It took me a while to sort this out.) Furthermore, Debra's father wanted Debra and her children to move out and had threatened to throw out her things. Finding affordable housing is very difficult, which made her situation even more precarious.

By the end of the first week of focusing on the *ohana* system of family values, Debra was still wondering how this training was rel-

MARYKNOLL SISTERS COMMUNICATIONS

Bitrina at work in the food pantry of a women's shelter in Hawaii.

evant to finding a job. I explained the important connections in her basic environment—between self and others and between family and work. I emphasized that unless we can see these connections in everything we do, there is no sense in trying to find a job.

By the time Debra completed three weeks of training, she was able to articulate and clarify what was important to her and her children and she was able to establish goals for herself and follow through on them. She realized that looking for a job was no longer her first priority. With my help, she developed plans for more education for herself and made this a top priority. She applied for financial aid and registered for the spring semester to complete her undergraduate degree at the University of Hawaii-Manoa. When she graduates she hopes to pursue another degree in English and eventually become a teacher. She's now a junior at the university and working part-time as a librarian. She hopes to move out from her father's house and support herself with her part-time job and some additional government support until she completes her education.

Debra was able to make it this far because she learned how to help herself. While Debra was attending our program, her children also received care from our agency. Low-income parents struggling to raise their children often need additional support. There were times when Debra was overwhelmed and frustrated. She was given parenting tips and regular weekly home visits to reduce the risk of child abuse. Now she sees clearly what she wants to accomplish and is working effectively on her goals.

I have not found this ministry easy. However, I am journeying with Debra and her children because I believe that all people I meet have dreams that are dear to their hearts. When some people who come to our center show progress in self-development and begin to live the *ohana* values, I am very grateful. I believe it is the steady encouragement, support, and love that make Debra able to clearly articulate her goals and to pursue her dreams. No matter where we come from or where we are now, we all need to love each other.

Only one thing sustains my mission work of relationships and that is my relationship with God. God has been and is the center of my life. God is my best friend and I communicate with God daily in many different ways. I watch the sunset and reflect on God's wonderful gift to me through nature. I share my experiences of God with people of different cultures and ethnicities. I communicate with God as I listen to music, write my journal, read Scripture, and quietly reflect on my daily activities. I communicate with God through our community prayer, where we all lift up our needs, the needs of our neighbors, and the needs of the world. And, of course, celebrating the Eucharist with my parish family is a great source of strength and helps keep me in mission. I find *ohana* in my parish.

My relationships with others also help sustain my mission work. Interests, crises, institutions, and organizations will come and go, but personal relationships will continue if we choose to sustain them. In order to relate to others effectively and to clarify my own values and beliefs, I must spend part of each day reflecting on who I am, why I am here, and where I am going. It is these beliefs and values that determine my actions in relating to others. These values did not begin when I entered Maryknoll. They were present even when I was a little girl. I knew even then that I had a fire in my heart to share what I had with others.

I was born in the small village of Nangwa in the northeast part of Tanzania. We were eight children, two boys and six girls. After secondary school, I attended a teacher training college in Arusha and then taught in primary schools and in an adult education program.

Although no one in my family or even my close friends ever thought I would become a religious Sister, I always wanted to help others. This call to serve others was nurtured by my parents and especially my grandmother, who lived with us. She saw goodness in every person and was always ready to reach out to others. She kept us children focused on our identity and reminded us continually of our values.

At the secondary school I had attended, run by the Maryknoll Sisters, the values taught by my grandmother had been reinforced by the way the Sisters lived and interacted with Tanzanians. Their service and total commitment really inspired me. The Sisters I met in Tanzania had within themselves an appreciation and respect for others as they were. They also seemed to have flexible dispositions willing to accommodate to cultural customs other than their own. They did not try to change our culture or our way of life but, instead, they adapted to them. This was a new experience for me because most missionaries who went to Tanzania not only kept their way of life, but also tried to change our customs to theirs.

As I had been growing up, then teaching and continuing my education, I knew something was missing in my life but I didn't know exactly what it was. After spending time reflecting and listening to my inner self, I felt a strong desire to respond in faith to a personal call from God to serve others. I decided to visit the Maryknoll Sisters. I made a first visit to their house in Tanzania and decided to live with them to see what their community life was like; within two weeks I loved their life style and wanted to become a Maryknoll Sister. They were such real people, with no pretenses. I saw them when they were happy or angry or disappointed. They lived their lives as God had created them, and I thought, that's what I want. Nothing else.

On August 21, 1988, I formally entered Maryknoll and then made my first profession of vows in New York on October 21, 1990. I received my first mission assignment to Hawaii the following year. I did not even know how to swim, yet here I was in the middle of the Pacific Ocean! I was frightened because I did not know another person in Hawaii. The only thing I had was the word of God. God told Abraham, "Go forth from the land of your kinsfolk and from your father's house to a land that I will show you" (Genesis 12:1-2). I firmly believe that God led me to Hawaii and responded in my heart, "Here I am Lord. I have come to do your will." When I arrived at Honolulu International Airport, I instinctively knew that I was making a journey that would shape my life.

During four years of pastoral work as director of religious education in a parish, I had become increasingly aware of the existence of violence within families. After working with some abused family members, I realized that I needed further training so I went back to school and completed a degree at Hawaii Pacific University.

My present ministry profits from my education and from my experience, but I continue to reach out for wisdom and understanding in order to be of service to others. I still have much to learn about Hawaiian culture and values and am grateful for the many people who share their values, beliefs, and lives with me. My life is continually being shaped by the diversity of cultures and ethnic groups in this land.

My vocation seems a call to constant transitions. It was hard to leave Tanzania, the places and people I love dearly, but part of my heart remains with them. My culture, reinforced by its traditions and practices, is what regenerates me and enables me to reach out to others. As I've moved from Tanzania to New York to Hawaii, I've been answering God's call. For me, the call is to be among strangers so that we will be strangers no more.

13

Falling in Love, Twice

Father Dennis Moorman

While I was working as a U.S. Peace Corps volunteer in Burkina Faso, a country nestled in the heart of West Africa, a six-year-old boy told me a story that caused me to reflect more critically on the world in which I was living. Yembuani (a name that in the Gulmancé language means "God loves me") would stop by my house every day just before going to school and right after coming home from school. I think that he must have found me entertaining—this strange foreigner who had recently moved to his small and isolated village. One day he was playing with a trinket that someone had sent me as a gift from the States when he expressed in amazement, "You white people can make anything!"

Reacting out of embarrassment, I said, "Oh, Yembuani, that's not true! Everyone is creative."

He replied, "Yes, it is true, my grandfather told me a story that proves it. When God was making the world, God told the people not to watch. In obedience, the black people covered their eyes. The white people pretended to cover their eyes, but they were really peeking through their fingers watching all that God was doing."

At first I was taken aback by this story, thinking about how white colonialism had stripped the African peoples of their self-esteem. But then I began to reflect upon the deeper truth expressed through his story. I saw how the story took into account the real existence of inequalities in the world and explained that privileges were somehow gained through cheating and injustice, which was a result of disobedience to God's will. Wow! The deep wisdom communicated through the mouth of this young boy overwhelmed me!

I grew up in a rural farming community in Decatur County in southeastern Indiana. Most of the people I knew growing up were descendants of German and Irish immigrants. I am a second-generation descendant of German immigrants to the U.S. I have two younger brothers and two younger sisters. My mother took care of us kids at home and my father worked in a factory to support us. The community in which I grew up was ethnically quite homogeneous. However, I was always interested in anyone I met from another culture. It was only after entering college at Purdue University in northwestern Indiana that I began to meet lots of people from many different countries. I especially enjoyed attending the international dinners given at the St. Thomas Aquinas Newman Center and talking with people from all parts of the world. After changing my major area of study several times, I finally graduated from Purdue in 1985 with a B.S. in agronomy (soil and crop science). It was fresh out of college that I decided to join the Peace Corps and work as a volunteer, helping small farmers improve their crop production and soil conservation techniques in West Africa.

Upon returning home to the United States after my two-year Peace Corps stint, I was surprised to find that it actually seemed more difficult to adjust back to the U.S. than it had been to adjust to the drastically different culture in Burkina Faso, living among the Gulmancé people. I had come back to complete a master's degree in plant physiology at North Carolina State University in Raleigh. In trying to adjust to life back home, I encountered the pain of trying to fit back in to a very individualistic, work-centered, and consumerist culture that was so different from the communitarian and people-centered focus on life that I had discovered in Burkina Faso. Near the completion of my master's degree, and while deciding whether to continue work on a doctorate, I realized that my heart had never really left Burkina Faso. Many of my friends at the university were people from other cultures or those who had lived and worked in other countries. I felt a strong draw to return to Africa, but how and doing what, I wasn't sure.

When I was fifteen years old, I had thought about the possibility of becoming a priest. It wasn't seen as too "cool" of a thing to do, so I had never said a word to anyone. But because the thought and desire had stayed with me for more than ten years, I decided "now" was the time to check it out and either act on it or put it to rest. I wrote to many different missionary organizations, especially those that worked exclusively in Africa, because that's where I wanted to go. Maryknoll was among the groups I contacted, but I wasn't seriously interested in them; knowing that they worked in Africa, Asia, and Latin America, I was afraid that I could be sent somewhere other than Africa. However, when I was invited to Maryknoll and sat around the dining room tables talking with veteran missionaries and listening to their stories, I felt so at home that I decided to seriously consider entering the Maryknoll seminary and studying to become a missionary priest.

What I find so ironic about my story is that falling in love with the Gulmancé people in West Africa was what stimulated me to search deeper within my heart for how I wanted to focus my life's journey. My desire had been expressed to return and live and work in Africa. But up until now, I haven't yet fulfilled that dream. Love, I have learned, can take many forms. Since ordination I have been living and working in South America with the Maryknoll Brazil Mission Community.

What attracted me to the Brazil Community was the idealism of the first paragraph of its mission vision: "We, members of the Brazil Mission Community, work to develop more life-giving structures, to live out a participative, collaborative and inter-vocational model of community among ourselves. Together, as equals,

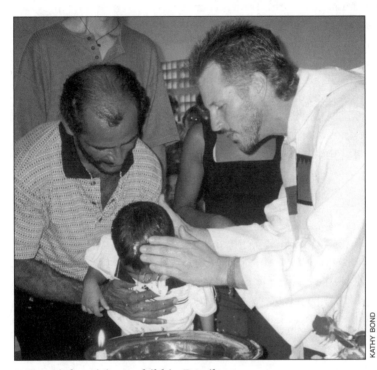

Dennis baptizing a child in Brazil.

we share ministry and mission through dialogue, partnership and celebration of life." Until this day, I still believe in this vision as an important way of being in mission and going about the transformation of our world. Trying to live this vision empowers me, gives me energy, and motivates me each day to continue to commit myself to the mission of Jesus Christ.

Here in Brazil we are a community of Maryknoll lay missioners (single and married, with and without children), priests and Sisters (Brothers have also been a part of our community). We don't necessarily live together in community, but we vision, reflect, and organize together, committing ourselves to support one another in the common missionary endeavor in which we all share.

As a member of the Maryknoll Brazil Mission Community, I am challenged to live out my priestly vocation authentically. The beauty of our community is that we have a variety of vocational charisms that complement and challenge one another. Being an ordained priest gives me a special responsibility to help all baptized people realize their own priestly vocation, which is conferred on them through baptism. For me, to be a priest is to be a special manifestation of God in our world, to be sacrament. I find that my challenge is to model this and help others to realize this in their own lives. So often, people want to see the priest as someone different from themselves, someone who is more holy or closer to God. I dislike being seen and treated as someone different. I want to show people that we are *all* special in God's eyes and that we each have a special part to play in building a better world. As an ordained priest I often have a sacred and special privilege of being called upon to be present with people at powerful and life-transforming moments throughout their life journeys. I love having the opportunity to try to help bring alive the sacraments and make them relevant to people's lives, when so often people are searching for something meaningful and nourishing to give them hope for something better.

I have fallen in love with Brazil, just as I had fallen in love with Africa. But I have also discovered Africa in Brazil through the more than 60 percent of the Brazilian population with African blood pumping through their veins. I meet Africa every day, not only in people's faces but in the music, dance, food, and spirituality of the Brazilian people. The Brazilian church is famous for implementing a theology of liberation, which initially developed from the poor Latin Americans' experience of oppression and their experience working for a transformed world preached by Jesus of Nazareth, called the reign of God.

In this spirit I would like to tell another true story from Burkina Faso that I feel expresses so well this vision of the reign of God to which we are committed as Catholic Christians. The story happened like this . . .

Soon after moving into my two-room, mud-brick house in the village of Pièla, I realized that I had moved into the section of town where many of the women who worked as prostitutes were also living. They were mostly foreigners like me. Despite this fact, a lot of neighborhood kids would often come and visit me. One day I started to play frisbee with a young boy who had stopped by for a visit. While we were playing, one of the young women who worked in a bar as a prostitute started watching us. After a little while, I threw the frisbee to her, and she joined in with our fun. Then a little while later, an old man came walking by and started watching us play. Pretty soon the young woman threw the frisbee to him. He dropped the frisbee and his cane too, but then clumsily picked the frisbee back up and threw it to the young boy. And there we were, the most unlikely mix of people in a little African village: an old man, a prostitute, a little boy, and a foreigner, all standing together in a circle, throwing a frisbee, and having fun together. When I reflected on this experience later, I realized that I had received a vision of what the reign of God is all about: love, equality, beauty, and enjoyment with no one excluded or left out.

14

From Law to Mission

Patrick Capuano

I should begin with the ending: while I am a corporate lawyer by training, I am a missioner at heart. While law was my job, mission is my call. Thankfully, my training in law has often been a tool that helps me live out my call. Mission—serving God and God's suffering children and striving joyfully (and sometimes striving to strive joyfully!) to share God's love and hope in an often difficult world—is my deeper vocation and my real life.

It has taken me a while to understand that these are different but not mutually exclusive ideas, and it has taken me even more time to appreciate what this means in my life. It has also taken time to figure out God's call. Along the way, I've tried to find the strength to live it as best as I can, celebrating when I do and not being too hard on myself when I can't. Mission seems to be the greatest thing in the world that I could possibly do with the gift of life that God has given me.

But that's now. I didn't always know this is what I wanted to do. The fourth of five children in a Catholic family of mixed Italian and East European descent, I was a pretty good student and relatively well behaved. I first attended public schools and then moved to parochial schools for seventh grade, and finished junior high and high school at an Opus Dei boys' school. I was not an altar boy, although many of my friends were.

I earned my B.A. at Johns Hopkins University in Baltimore, not far from where I grew up in Washington, D.C. I spent five years at Johns Hopkins, interrupting my liberal arts studies for a one-year tour as a Russian "voice language analyst" for the National Security Agency. I made many friends among these intriguing, dedicated, and talented people, including several Mormons who were in the same program. I was moved by their faith and drawn to them by their ease in talking about it. It struck a chord I did not identify at the time.

After graduating from Hopkins in 1986, I applied to law school, along with many of my friends. Although I'd majored in creative writing, it was an easy decision because my father, older brother, and one older sister are also lawyers. Off I went to the University of Virginia.

I was not always a religious person. This certainly was not the fault of my parents. We went to church every Sunday and all the holy days, even when we were on vacation. My parents taught me to say my prayers every night. Most of the time I did, but sometimes I didn't. As I got older, the "didn't" times began to outnumber the "dids." When I entered my late teens and twenties and could choose whether or not to attend church, Sunday mass was often sacrificed. Some months I attended Sunday mass regularly and other months I skipped mass for weeks at a time. There seemed to be so many other things to do. (If God was calling me then, I just wasn't picking up the signals!)

Toward the end of law school, I had begun to think more about faith, belief, and God. Why? At the time, I didn't know; it was just a feeling. Perhaps part of the reason was that I was nearing the end of my law school career and I was a little scared and unsure of what might come next. I started going to church again. Some of my friends had stopped going to church because they didn't feel it offered them much and said that the preaching didn't really speak to their lives.

Since I had determined to be faithful, I decided that it wasn't the preacher who was speaking to me, it was God speaking *through* the preacher. I believed that if I went to church and visited God in God's house, then God was going to talk to me. I just had to be willing to receive. Usually, it was nothing too life-changing, perhaps a small bit of enlightenment, a new way of seeing a reading that made it meaningful, that helped me work out a personal quandary. The feeling of knowing that God was with me was comforting. It was a small taste of what was to come. Although I still wasn't "there," I could feel I was getting closer to what I sought and, at the time, that was enough.

Not long after, during my last year of law school, I was in front of my house, taking the strings of multicolored lights out of a tall evergreen, when something happened that made me stop and think. A friend and I were talking about what we wanted after law school, about our future careers as lawyers. She asked me what I wanted to be and I said spontaneously, "a saint, I want to be a saint." She obviously thought this was weird. That's fine for a kid to say, but I was in my twenties, headed for a job with a major law firm. When she asked me to clarify what I meant, I thought and then simply repeated it. She left me by myself to finish untangling my Christmas lights. To tell the truth, I was a little surprised myself at how quickly my answer came out. Still, I was surprised about how right and comfortable it felt.

Three years later, at age twenty-six, I graduated and moved to Los Angeles. Several of my friends were moving west, and I thought I might have the chance to write. I felt that I had made it! Good job, great friends, cool town! What wasn't there to like? What not to be happy about?

But deep down, I wasn't happy. I socialized a lot, went out for dinner, barbecued with friends. I had a couple of serious romantic relationships. It seemed a good life: it was fun and lucrative. But what was missing?

I began work in a corporate law firm in the area of real estate. I prepared contracts for senior associates, who revised my drafts for review by low-level partners, and so on up the law-firm food chain. I hunkered down and worked very hard. Like most people,

Lay missioner Pat giving out school books and clothes to orphan boys at Wat Prok Temple in Bangkok.

I had a desire not to do harm. At first, this was fine. Then when I was assigned to draft a contract so one company could buy a shopping center, tearing down an old center to replace it with a new one, I asked myself what I was doing. In itself, it wasn't a bad thing, and it could have good benefits for workers in the stores, but it made me think: I may have been avoiding doing harm, but was I doing any good, anything worthwhile?

At the time I was doing some work for Catholic Charities but still felt like I wasn't really engaged in life. I was living on the edges, eating the cooled soup from the edges of the bowl rather than digging right in, maybe getting a little burned but going for the solid stuff. A New Testament story haunted me: was I burying my talents in the dirt? I started to realize that my talents went beyond my legal skills to the life God gave to me. Practicing law, even *pro bono*, wasn't enough. I wanted to do good, and not just *not* do bad.

I still didn't move. I wasn't all that unhappy. I just didn't know how happy I could be. Then things began to happen. I began to pray more and found a new church with a great music program. Then I lost my job because of an economic downturn in Los Angeles. Finally, in 1992 Los Angeles experienced a major riot with burning and looting.

While I was looking for another job in law, a Jewish friend asked if I would help her collect canned goods to take to the inner city where the damage and needs were the greatest. She was a municipal employee who developed social outreach programs for inner-city youth. Although she comes from a wealthy family, she dedicates her life to this; it is her full-time job. I thought what a good way to spend your life.

I found a new job, but really wasn't happy. Something, I thought, was going on, something had to change. I began to pray for guidance, always asking God to show me the way. I wondered why God wasn't helping me. I finally concluded that I knew what I really wanted to do with my life—and what God wanted—but that I just wasn't doing it. It's one thing *not* to know, but it's quite another to know and not do. Knowledge brings responsibility to act on that knowledge. I was simply afraid of making the change.

I felt called to enter into full-time service to and for the poor. I knew I wanted to serve overseas working with people who had few options, and I wanted to do this with a church group. I wanted to dedicate myself to a life of relatively limited means, living my life for others and living it for God.

Nervously, I mentioned this to a few friends. They thought I was a little "off the deep end," but they still supported me. I didn't tell my family because I didn't want them to worry. I researched some organizations and finally decided to apply to Maryknoll. Although I was beyond the deadline for applications, I was determined because I knew this was where I belonged. When I contacted Maryknoll's admissions team, they agreed to let me be interviewed at their house in Los Angeles. I moved more quickly than I have ever moved in my life. For the first time, it felt like I was starting to live the life I was meant to live.

Maryknoll turned out to be a perfect fit for me. First, I wanted a chance to spend significant time with local people rather than be placed in an office job or administrative post far from the reality of people in need. Maryknoll requires every new missioner to spend at least six months in full-time language study so they are prepared to make friends and to share the joys and struggles of life with the poorest of the poor.

I was also looking for a chance to work alongside priests, Brothers, and Sisters as equals. Maryknoll's structure encourages this, and its lay mission program includes experienced life-long missioners, couples, and even families. Finally, Maryknoll encourages each missioner to integrate faith, spirituality, peace and justice work, pastoral work, and ecumenical outreach to nurture a truly holistic mission life.

When I joined Maryknoll I knew only that I wanted to serve the poor of this world. When I arrived in Cambodia, I was encouraged to respond fully to my call. God was definitely at work in Cambodia. Maryknoll asked me to work with people, which was what I had requested. There was an outreach program to older people who were blind, but we also wanted to start a skill-training program for young adults. Many were fully capable of holding jobs, but because they were blind their parents, and Cambodia's social mores, kept them locked away at home. We knew they were capable of more and we wanted to support them. When I was asked to initiate the program, knowing nothing about what was involved, I accepted, putting my confidence in God!

God did a great job. I did preliminary research and we began a small program teaching basic music, Braille, and literacy skills. We really wanted to start a massage training program so these young adults could gain enough skills to earn income. Few people, including some Western "experts," gave it much chance of succeeding. The plan stalled for months because we couldn't find a teacher. Then shortly after we had started the basic teaching program, a new student enrolled. Although not completely blind, he wanted to study. Soon after, he asked if a cousin of his visiting from Canada could see the program. The cousin, who was also blind, wanted to stay with us. He had been trained in Japan as a masseur, and for the previous twenty years had worked in a massage-therapy clinic in Quebec. In addition, he spoke Khmer (for teaching students and soothing doubtful parents), English, French, and Japanese, and he knew how to run a business. He knew the culture of Khmers so he could teach appropriately and he also knew the culture of Westerners so he could teach our students how to treat any Western clients. And he was an excellent role model—a successful blind Cambodian with a family. Our prayers had been answered.

One day as I watched him at a "question and answer" meeting for prospective students and their parents, I saw how he brought hope to the parents and enthusiasm to the students. His words carried unexpected hopes and dreams to people who didn't dare to hope or dream. I sat off to one side and watched the meeting unfold. I realized that my most "important" role might be just to be a warm body, a medium through which God can work in the world. Because I was there, we started a program, a student showed up, a cousin visited. My role was just to be there, and God did the rest. I started to develop my own spirituality, the spirituality of being what I call a "utility player," someone willing to try almost anything in order to plant a seed that God can nourish.

I worked with the massage program for a couple of years and then turned it over to another Maryknoller when I felt a strong call to begin human rights work. Seng Phally, a Cambodian who directed a small labor rights organization, taught me about the issues that were important to factory workers in Cambodia. That work brought me many gifts, including the opportunity to help workers directly in many ways. My language skills seemed a mixed blessing. It is one thing to read a report in English, typed and bound, about suffering many miles away. It is quite another to sit and face the people who are suffering and learn directly from them about their lives. But it is also a blessing to be there, to listen, and to be able to say, "I hear what you are saying, I care, and I am going to help you any way I can."

My work with the labor-rights organization called me to be a voice for the voiceless, representing their needs to appropriate Cambodian, American, or company officials. I also helped the voiceless to gain their own voice. Maryknoll provided funds for workshops, English-language training, and even overseas exposure trips so that the workers can represent themselves in the years to come.

Living in Cambodia, a predominantly Buddhist country, has given me a greater understanding of my own faith. When Christmas is just another day of the week, for example, I find myself reflecting more deeply on its meaning. There are also many opportunities for interfaith dialogue, even on a personal level. One Sunday, my friend Phally asked if he could attend the local Christian church with me, which made me very happy. Afterwards, we went to eat breakfast together (Cambodian rice-noodle soup) and he explained how amazed he was that Khmer parents brought young children to the service, that it was conducted in the local language, and that the people were actively participating by singing and reading and praying. All this was different from the prayers at his Buddhist temple, where revered monks recite prayers in the old Pali language, not understood by most Cambodians, and children are left at home.

Phally helped me appreciate my religion, and perhaps his experience will help him encourage the leaders of his Buddhist temple to invite more participation by people in those services. As we say in Cambodia, it's just as important to have good Buddhists as it is to have good Christians. Sharing helps everyone.

Maryknoll and the Cambodian people have helped me see and understand the world in a new way. It is alive, joyful, full of great need, and full of people—from the West and the East—struggling together to improve it through action and through prayer. Because it is impossible to *un*-know something—whether it is an injustice or a moment of shared joy—the world is a different place than it was before. It is different because I learned, and different because I struggled alongside.

And so I will end with the beginning: I am a lawyer by trade, but I am a missioner at heart. I learned this on my journey to Cambodia. As a missioner, my responsibility in life is to respond as best as I can—to God and to the needs of people. This journey of discovery and learning, about myself and God, continues.

15

If I Don't Have Love,
I Am Nothing, Lord

Sister Mary Mullady

One of the favorite hymns in Guatemala, "*Si yo no tengo amor, yo nada soy, Señor*" (If I don't have love, I am nothing, Lord), captures the story of why I'm living in El Quetzal, Guatemala, as a Maryknoll Sister. It is this love that is the foundation of my life as a missioner and the reason why I live in this city of 90,000, an hour away from Guatemala City.

We live with very little, but have a great deal of love surrounding us. Our city is made up mostly of Kaqchikel Indians whose ancestors have lived here for four generations and Ladinos, *mestizos* who speak Spanish who have recently arrived from poorer parts of the country to find work. The needs here seem almost overwhelming at times—jobs, health care, public transportation, running water, education—very basic things. We try to find solutions together, praying together, reflecting on the Scriptures, and through caring and loving one another.

My journey to the Maryknoll Sisters didn't take the form of a dramatic "call," but, instead, was a gradual process. I was born in New York City, in Queens, in a family of nine girls. As the oldest, I babysat, changed diapers, and did lots of household chores. My father was a police officer and my mother took care of us children, which was more than a full-time job! We children attended a Catholic grammar school that was so strict that I was actually afraid of my teachers during the first years. I was a good student and liked reading, history, and geography. I remember getting a Christmas gift one year of a set of books about different countries. The pictures of people living in foreign countries were exciting. I wondered why they lived so differently than we did. I wondered what their lives were like.

My family prayed together and we always attended mass on Sundays. I perceived God as a gentle man and was attracted to saints like Bernadette of Lourdes and Thérèse of Lisieux, who seemed to have magical powers. As I grew older, I began to experience God as a Spirit who was always with me on my journey.

I grew up during the 1960s and 1970s, a tumultuous time of social change. When John F. Kennedy was assassinated, I was in first grade and heard the announcement come over the school's public address system. I knew something awful had happened to President Kennedy, even though I didn't understand the word "assassinated." My fears were confirmed when my mother came to school to pick me up instead of letting me take the bus home, which is what I normally did. As we walked home, I saw she had been crying. Kennedy's assassination left me shaken. Despite my young age, I became politically conscious and understood the words "segregation," "civil rights," and "desegregation." I was aware that the people in my neighborhood were white and that an invisible line separated the white and the black communities. When I walked through the black community, people stared at me, and when a black person walked through our neighborhood, we stared at him or her.

One of the happiest memories of my childhood was when I was in fifth grade and made the swim team sponsored by the Catholic Youth Organization. (It makes me smile even today.) I had pleaded with one of my sisters to come with me to the try-outs and that evening we watched girls diving in the water and skill-

Surrounded by children, Mary finds joy among
Guatemalans.

fully swimming laps. My sister and I looked at each other dumb-founded. We could barely swim. When it was our turn, we jumped into the water and struggled anxiously to make it to the end of the pool. The happiest day of my young life was when the coach looked down at us and shouted, "OK, you're on the team!"

After finishing Catholic grammar school, I went to the nearby public school. The population was much more diverse culturally and racially than at the Catholic school. My grades were only fair as I barely studied at all. I had lost interest in school except for history and English. I was very surprised to receive a high grade for a term paper I did on migrant workers. My very basic research made me aware for this first time of the terrible and unjust conditions migrants suffered. At someone's suggestion I read *The Grapes of Wrath* by John Steinbeck and became completely absorbed by the plight of the Joad family. When I read *The Jungle* by Upton Sinclair, I was astonished by the working conditions in the factories. Although I didn't realize it at the time, this must have been a turning point in my life.

During my teenage years, I was quiet and shy and preferred to go to movies, concerts, or dances in groups. I liked Simon and Garfunkel and Tracy Chapman. I went to foreign films because the photography was beautiful and they seemed to give a broader perspective about life. I attended Queens College, part of the City University of New York, and took liberal arts courses that interested me. I had no particular career in mind and, like many of my peers, I wasn't worried about finding a full-time job. I dated more frequently, and our home on weekends—with nine sisters coming and going—was a small circus. This was a time of racial tensions, drug use, and the beginnings of the sexual revolution, but our parents had strict rules about being home at a certain time, which helped us cope with all these changes.

After graduating from college with a major in English, I worked in Manhattan as a secretary. My jobs were interesting but not challenging in any way. When there was a shortage of teachers in the Brooklyn diocese, I sent in my resume and was immediately hired to teach fifth- and sixth-graders, with many of them immigrant children from Latin America. I attended classes at night to get my teaching certificate and moved into my own apartment.

I liked having my summers free so I could travel or volunteer with summer projects. Two experiences sponsored by religious groups exposed me to poverty situations. At the first, in Los Angeles, we worked with children at risk in an area controlled by a number of warring gangs. The children did remedial work in the mornings and in the afternoons we took them on trips to the beach, Disneyland, and Hollywood. When we visited their homes, we often saw two or three families living together. Because the parents worked long hours, the children were frequently alone. The gangs, divided along racial lines, offered protection.

The other experience was in Florida. We spent time with migrant workers who worked in the fields. We also visited their homes and spent one incredibly difficult day picking tomatoes with them. What arduous work it was! There were no hot showers to rinse off the dust and dirt. Later, I felt even worse when I heard that the fields were often sprayed with pesticides, exposing the workers to contamination.

I sensed that God was calling me to religious life, but, honestly, I didn't want to respond. One time I did go to a discernment weekend sponsored by the diocese, but it provided little help. Then one day when I was reading *Maryknoll* magazine, I saw a small form used to inquire about vocations, cut it out, and mailed it. At the time I wasn't even sure why I did this. As a result, I was invited to a "sharing weekend" at the Maryknoll Sisters' Center in Ossining, New York. This was another turning point for me. The Sisters were friendly and their mission charism was evident. But I was scared. I prayed to God for the courage to do what was best for me and told only a few close friends and my parents that I was thinking about joining the Maryknoll Sisters. I finally made the big decision, not completely sure I was doing the right thing.

After living by myself, the first experiences of community were difficult, but the Sisters were very patient. The other candidates, who were from Asia, Africa, and Latin America, brought their different cultures and customs, including new forms of prayer, which challenged and stretched me. I still missed my family and friends and wondered if I had made the right choice. Once I arrived in Guatemala, my country of choice, my doubts disappeared.

My time in Guatemala has been life-giving. Yes, there have been situations and events that seemed hopeless or nerve-racking. Once, when I was on an overcrowded bus going back home, our driver decided to race another bus. The drivers became angrier with each other and for twenty minutes the buses careened around dangerous curves in the road, trying to cut each other off. Passengers yelled and screamed, and I felt sick. At the first chance, I got off the bus and walked all the way home.

One family I visited lived in a one-room house with the roof and walls covered with tin and cardboard, a typical home for poor Guatemalans. During the rainy season the roof leaked and the floor was always covered with mud. One day while I was visiting there was a rainstorm. Outside, the rain gushed down the street and water dripped into the house through the roof. The little boy told me I would have to stay the night. I smiled at the invitation, knowing I'd be very uncomfortable. Why did people have to live in such wretched conditions?

Many factors cause poverty, including discrimination and inadequate education. People's lives are made even more difficult by a lack of health care and inadequate diets. Even worse is the lack of employment opportunities. The few low-paying jobs that are available often result from the globalization of industry. A seventeen-year-old girl told me of her experience working in a factory. She works six days a week at very low wages, with a director who can hit the workers. They have a short lunch break, but when I asked her about coffee breaks, she had no idea what I was talking about. (This struck me as particularly odd, as for over a hundred years coffee was a major export of Guatemala!)

In Guatemala, the women go to the market daily to buy food, they wash clothes by hand, and they usually prepare meals over an open fire. Most women must also collect wood and carry water. One day when I was driving our jeep, I saw a young girl I knew carrying a pile of wood on top of her head. I stopped and offered to drive her home. However, her load was so heavy that I couldn't even lift the wood off her head. I had to let her continue on her slow journey.

What sustains me in my mission work? Prayer, writing letters, living in community, and being thankful to God. I live with another Maryknoll Sister and we share a life of community as well as the challenges of living our vows of chastity, poverty, and obedience. Despite the poverty that surrounds us, we see daily the beauty of Guatemala, the Mayan ruins, its rich farmlands, beautiful cities, and volcanoes. We enjoy meals of *tortillas, frijoles, piñol,* and fresh fruit.

While our poverty doesn't equal that of the Guatemalan people, we experience their frustrations with inadequate transportation, the constant shortage of water, and increasing crime. Every morning I go to a nearby Catholic church to meet with a group of women who read the gospel of the day and say the rosary. We pray together for the overwhelming needs of our community, including unemployment and sickness. In our Bible-reflection group we discuss these realities and how they relate to the Bible. At times like this, my spirits soar with the faith of the people. I feel as if I'm part of one of the children's favorite celebrations when they make kites and fly them in the cool breezes on All Souls Day. They fly their kites high so they might reach their loved ones in heaven. As their love rises high, I think again of "*Si yo no tengo amor.*" Love is something eternal that will never pass away. It is what sustains my mission journey as a Maryknoll Sister.

16

God Is Drawing Me In
Like a Breath

Father Joseph Everson

So there I was, a one-time successful attorney sitting on a hillside overlooking Lake Titicaca, waiting to begin a eucharistic service. How did I get from the canyons of Wall Street to the Altiplano of Peru?

I'll never forget that cold February morning in 1997 when I left the rectory to go out and serve one of the rural communities of our parish. I was working in the town of Yunguyo. I had been assigned there as a seminarian for two and a half years as part of Maryknoll's overseas training program. That day started off like any other, but I still had not yet learned that in mission nothing stays the same.

February is part of the rainy season in the Altiplano and it had been especially heavy that year. The small bus left me off along the main road, and I began trudging up the hillside through the mud. Since I was already at an altitude of 12,500 feet, the hike was difficult, and it was made worse by the lack of a path. I finally made it to the house and after greeting the family I sat down on a rock outside to catch my breath and wait for the others to arrive. I sat there and thought about the life I left behind when I entered the seminary. I remembered my job as a corporate attorney at a high-powered Manhattan law firm—going to work in suits and working late into the night, if not through the night, on large corporate deals. I recalled my apartment on Roosevelt Island overlooking the bright lights of Manhattan. Most of all, I thought about my friends and all the pleasant experiences we shared in New York City. Then I looked around at the potato fields, the gray skies, the scattered adobe houses, and I asked God, "Where are you in all of this?"

Reflecting on that moment, it's a wonder I ever managed to make it to that house on the hillside. They say the shortest distance between two places is a straight line. Well, I've never been good with directions, so I suppose I took one of the longer, more winding roads to get there.

I was born and raised the youngest of ten children (six boys and four girls) in a working-class neighborhood of San Francisco. My father was a fireman and my mother a nurse, both devout Catholics. I attended Catholic schools and this is where my interest in the priesthood first sprouted. I had been fortunate in knowing some outstanding men who were priests, first at our local parish and later at my Jesuit high school. Their kindness and dedication greatly impressed me and touched something within me that desired the same life for myself.

By the time I graduated from high school in 1980, young men were no longer entering directly into the seminary. I decided to put the thought of a vocation aside and go to college. I majored in history at the University of California at Berkeley. It didn't take long between making new friends, studying, working, and intramural sports for me to forget the idea of becoming a priest. But God was waiting for me, and during my junior year I felt the desire not just to become a priest, but to become a missioner as well. I already knew about Maryknoll from the magazine my parents received at home. However, something within me was not yet ready to make a commitment. I wasn't sure if this life was for me and at that time I was searching for an absolute certainty that I would never find. So off to law school I went, although I had never given much thought to being an attorney either!

It was while I was working as a corporate attorney for Skadden, Arps in New York City that I once again found God patiently waiting for me. I enjoyed my work at the firm, but I knew it was not what I wanted for the rest of my life. By this time I was subscribing to *Maryknoll* magazine for myself. When I read it each month, I was so impressed by the stories of the missioners that my missionary priesthood vocation again rose up within me. I decided it was "now or never." I was concerned that I might become attached to the generous salary and benefits of working for a large corporate law firm and that if I did not take the chance and enter Maryknoll at that time, my vocation might die. So even with some uncertainty and ambiguity about where all this might lead, I followed my instincts, placed my trust in God, and entered Maryknoll.

One of my formators in the seminary told me that mission is like breathing—there are times when God draws us in and times when God sends us out. When I first joined Maryknoll it was a time of being drawn in by God. In the seminary I found my relationship with God and my prayer life growing in unimaginable ways from the start. I received support from the other men with whom I lived in community. But it was not a time to focus on myself as a goal; rather, it was all preparation for being sent out as a missioner and standing before God on my own two feet.

My first placement was in that town of Yunguyo high in the Peruvian Altiplano. I had asked to work there because it was a predominantly rural area and, being from a large city, I wanted to see if I could survive in a rural environment. It was there that I encountered the Aymara people for the first time. I had heard many other missioners say how hard it was to enter into ministry with the Aymara people because of the nature of their culture. But I didn't experience it that way. From the very beginning, they welcomed me into the parish and into their lives. My work varied quite a bit that first year. I was involved in much catechetical work

Joe, with a couple of young friends in the Andes.

with children and youth. I joined one of the nuns in the parish in running a Saturday afternoon program for children from first to sixth grade. It quickly swelled to about one hundred kids who came each Saturday for games, songs, reflections, and stories. What surprised me was how much enthusiasm the children had for acting out stories from the Bible.

I also worked quite a bit with our Christian Friendship Groups—a parish renewal program. These were groups within the various barrios of the town or the rural communities in which members would voluntarily get together once or twice a month to read the Bible, pray together, and concern themselves with those most disadvantaged among them. I found it an honor to be present among them. It never ceased to amaze me how well they could share their feelings about the ways the Bible spoke to them.

In all the various activities, however, nothing impressed me more than the Aymara people's way of seeing faith as an intrinsic part of their everyday life. This was most evident in the way religious practices accompanied much of their agricultural cycle. I remember one day in particular; it was the Monday before Ash Wednesday, known in Yunguyo as Jatakatu. I had gotten to know one family in town fairly well and they invited me to accompany them out to their fields. We left around mid-morning for the short trip. We found a place in the middle of the fields where we could sit down together. Then I went out with one of the men and we started to dig up a few of the potatoes. We did the same with each of the other crops and then placed all the products together on one of the traditional Aymara cloths. We lay colored streamers and confetti around them and sprinkled wine over them. We gathered together to pray and give thanks to God for the crops and to ask that there be a good harvest for all. After the prayers we stayed out in the fields listening to music and celebrating until the sun set.

I truly appreciated that day with that family. When they asked me to share in their celebration, I felt that they were inviting me into a deeper part of their lives. Mission for me is not leaving behind relationships I have with family and friends in the States. It is not substituting new people for old. Rather, it is casting an ever-widening circle so that others can be included with those to whom I am already close! It is a calling to open myself up more and more toward new peoples and customs without losing the ones that I bring with me.

After returning to the States to finish my theological studies, I was ordained a priest and reassigned to work in Peru. With ordination I found that nothing changed and yet everything changed. This time I was assigned to work in the southern city of Tacna, located near the coast and the Chilean border. It is a city of about 220,000 people, many of whom are Aymara migrants who have left the Altiplano in search of jobs and better schools for their children.

When I was talking with people in the diocese about what I might be able to offer, it turned out that a priest was urgently needed to join the team of lay men and women who were working in the prisons. Prison ministry is not something I had originally thought of. The famous Sing Sing Prison is located in the same area as Maryknoll and when I would hear of a few Maryknollers helping out there I always thought it was a ministry I could not personally do; I felt it would be too difficult. However, over time I came to know a Maryknoll priest who helped out in Chicago's Cook County jails a couple of days a week. I was impressed by the spiritual formation he did within the jails and the stories he would tell about his work there. Slowly I became open to the idea, even though I knew prison ministry would be a real challenge. So, by the time I arrived in Tacna, I was able to say, yes, I would give prison ministry a try. After all, mission involves being open not only to new cultures and peoples, but also to new challenges that call me to grow in my dependence on God. It has been one of the more important decisions I have made.

I have found few things as life-giving to me as prison ministry. Just outside the city of Tacna, there are two prisons, one for men and the other for women. Each week I spend one day in each prison and I have been pleasantly surprised at how receptive the prisoners are to me. After demonstrating a commitment by returning each week, we soon developed a trust and confidence between us. Although I am an attorney, I do no legal work in the jails. Rather, most of my time is spent with one-on-one spiritual and human formation. I hear confessions, listen to problems, and talk about difficulties they face within the prison and with their families. What I note more and more in working in the prisons is the very real conversion that goes on in the lives of many. For the first time many of the men and women are reflecting on their lives, on their character, and on God. It is with much humility that I accept their invitation to join them in their reflection.

Additionally, I run a sacramental preparation course for those who have not been baptized, confirmed, or received first communion. Although the group is small in each prison, it is filled with those who have an enthusiasm for learning more about our Catholic faith. The prison ministry also goes on outside the prison walls. Many of the prisoners, especially those who have not received visitors in a while, ask me to visit their families, spouses, and children. The families of the prisoners suffer when a loved one is incarcerated and this can be both an emotional and economic burden. So many of them carry a burden of shame, and these home visits can be important moments to further healing and reconciliation.

Our diocese is also home to Peru's most notorious prison, located in Challapalca. This prison is meant to be a place of punishment for the worst criminals, who are sent there for three years before being transferred to another prison. Challapalca is completely isolated, with the closest public transportation about forty miles away. It is located on an army base at an altitude of more than 15,000 feet. Although it is difficult to get there, I try to visit for a few days every other month.

Life is hard in Challapalca. The altitude and the extreme cold make it a miserable place, not just for the prisoners but for anyone connected to the prison, including the administration, guards, and soldiers. My first visits there did not go well. At first the director wouldn't allow me past his office. But I have learned in mission to be patient in many ways, with others and with myself. And so I continued to return to show my determination and concern, not just for the prisoners, but also for those who work in the prison. It is part of a willingness to serve all. Eventually, I was allowed not just inside the prison but into the cellblocks and given permission to talk with the prisoners in private. This was a big step forward for the prison ministry.

You can see the prisoners' appreciation of visits on their faces. Visits by family and friends are allowed only once a month. However, due to the isolated nature of this particular prison, most have never received a visit from family members or friends. Hiring a special car to take them there and back is too expensive for most. So I bring with me the knowledge that I am the only outsider visitor most of them receive. Our time together passes so quickly that I feel bad for not being able to stay longer or to visit more often. It is times like these that I also need to accept my limitations as a priest and a missioner and place a deeper trust in God. But I never allow my limitations to keep me from dreaming of all the possibilities that lie ahead for the prisoners and for this ministry.

I have also experienced the need to deal with limitations in my work with high-risk persons. Our diocese also has a mission to reach persons on the margins of society, such as addicts, prostitutes, and those with AIDS or who are HIV positive. Unfortunately, this ministry was not well organized when I arrived, and I was asked to try and get it off the ground. I discovered that forming a team to reach out to those on the margins is not easy. Peruvian society is still closed to them in many ways. Thus far, we have only started a ministry to help people who have AIDS, as well as their families. So much more is possible in this area, but I must rely on patience and confidence in God to see how it will unfold, not in my time but in God's time—always trusting in the sometimes slow but always sure work of God.

It is that trust in God that sustains me as a priest and especially as a missioner. I seem to be much less capable in the missions than in the States. Working in a new language and operating within different cultural norms and ways of thinking limit my abilities. I am no longer the self-confident attorney who customarily relied on himself alone to get the job done. Now, at times, I experience myself as unsure or hesitant about tasks I would have easily accomplished in the States.

It is during these moments that I am called to put a deeper trust in God. I ask God for the grace to set aside my anxieties and doubts—in effect, to set aside my ego—so that I can get on with the task at hand. I may not speak as eloquently in Peru or even be able to understand fully all that is said and done in my presence, but I can offer myself in service to others, trusting that God will provide me with what I need. And it is this same trust that becomes an interior anchor for me, giving me the stability I need while I move between countries, cultures, and customs.

So whenever I think back on that time when I sat on a rock outside the house on the hillside in Yunguyo, and other experiences like it, I realize that those are the moments when God is drawing me in like a breath to bring me closer. They are graced moments that help me remain faithful to my calling as a priest and as a missioner even as I live with the ambiguities such a life entails. And when God sends me out again, it is with a surer foundation to enable me to cast ever wider my circle of relationships in Peru and beyond. I am glad to be a missioner!

17

Dreaming

Sister Leonor Montiel

Telling the stories of three young people I work with seems to be the best way of telling my story. Today we all live in Cambodia, which is where our stories have become intertwined.

Srey Aem is a nineteen-year-old woman who wants to learn how to measure so that she will be able to learn to sew and thus earn money to help her family. She is in the fourth grade. Srey Aem is the oldest of six children in a family that lives in rural Cambodia. Her mother and the other children work on a farm, while her father stays at home, drinks himself into stupor, and then fights with his wife when she returns home. It is almost a miracle that Srey Aem is able to go back to school this year. Her parents are opposed because it means losing valuable helping hands.

Lot's story is quite different. After finishing college, he began work with a local non-government organization that does resource development for young people. His work taught him a great deal about human rights, human development, equality, and justice, and he committed himself to these values. Little did he know that these newly found beliefs would be soon tested. He fell in love with a handicapped woman who was not a virgin. Because such a marriage was not at all acceptable for a young, handsome, educated Khmer man, Lot's family totally opposed it. Newly con-scienticized about human rights, justice, and equality, Lot struggled with his conscience, with tradition, with family, but in the end, his family won. Lot was very sad and disappointed but he realized that he felt better because he now knew what was just, what was right, and that he had fought for it. Now he dreams that his children will be free to marry whomever they love.

Cenon, a twenty-year-old man in the ninth grade came to talk with me. "Bong Srey" (older sister), he said, "I have no goals." It was time to return to school and we were talking about resolutions and hopes for the school year. I told him that I was not talking about big hopes or life goals, but simpler things like good grades or no absences. But Cenon was adamant, "I'm not hoping for anything this school year," he said. Later he took me aside and explained, "I'm sorry but I dare not dream at all. My life has been full of disappointments. *Not* hoping lessens the impact of life's hardships."

Cenon's life has been like a series of derailed dreams. He was born in a refugee camp in Thailand to parents fleeing the war in Cambodia. They were hoping for resettlement to another country. Instead they were repatriated, with a promise of a free, happy family life, farming their own land in their native Cambodia. It didn't turn out that way, however. Family troubles broke the family up. They are now scattered all over Cambodia, with two younger siblings in an orphanage, their mother in and out of various relationships, and their father unheard of. Cenon is left alone without a home. "Tell me, Sister, how can I dare to dream?" he asked me.

Srey Aem, Lot, and Cenon are just three of the Cambodian youths I am working with in Cambodia as a Maryknoll Sister. In their struggles to find their rightful places in the world, or just to believe that they have a rightful place in the world to dream, to hope, and to be, I am also following a dream. My dream is of God's reign fulfilled here on earth—a reign where everyone believes and is treated as if he or she were God's beloved, made in the image and likeness of God.

MARYKNOLL SISTERS

Len enjoying a meal with students from Maryknoll's training program for disabled victims of land mines and polio in Phnom Penh.

My full name is Maria Leonor Falcutila Montiel, but I'm better known as Len. I am from the Philippines. I've not always been sure about my dreams and I certainly haven't always dreamed of the reign of God. At different points in my life, I hoped and dreamed like Srey Aem, Lot, and Cenon. Sometimes everything seemed simple and clear and other times I was ready to give up, just like Cenon. My dreams included going to the moon, winning the Tour de France, being a famous foreign correspondent, being "knock-out" gorgeous, having long beautiful legs, and so on. But it was the dream I almost gave up—my dream of the reign of God—that gave me so much hope.

My dream of the reign of God is a world where every creature is respected and has its own place, where peace, justice, and equality prevail, and where love reigns. This sounded—and sounds—very good to me. But growing up in a world full of "isms," not the least of which are materialism, cynicism, and capitalism, I thought this dream would remain just that, a dream. Was this ideal just that, an ideal, a good concept with nice words, or could it actually be lived? I was sure that to survive and thrive in the world, I would have to join the crowd and let go of my dream.

My dream began way back in my childhood in Looc, Romblon, a small town on a small island in the heart of the Philippines. I was born to a family with a proud heritage passed on from the time of Spanish colonization. My family's pride bordered on arrogance and, yes, we owned land with tenant farmers. We also had a faithful practice of religion, participating in endless masses, novenas, and processions, all of which were meant to make us better Christians. I learned early on that we are all brothers and sisters in Jesus Christ and we must love one another.

At the same time, I learned that as a child I always had to defer to the opinions of my elders, even if I thought otherwise. Many times I watched silently as an aunt scolded our old tenants like children because they had arrived late for the Good Friday procession. All I could think was that these poor folks had walked through the hilly terrain for at least two hours under the hot sun, without food (it was a day of fasting), and that soon they would be carrying Mary Magdalene's platform, the saint our family patronizes on Good Friday. The farmers usually wore old tattered clothes while the statue of Mary Magdalene shimmered in silk and velvet, with matching pearl or diamond earrings, and her own special expensive perfume. To my young mind, this didn't appear to be the way to love one another, but voicing such an opinion would have been the same as heresy, and I would have been roundly scolded.

For me, Holy Week, the time to remember Jesus' unconditional love and saving grace for all of us, became a time of rude awakening to the reality of the world's unfairness and of my place in it. It was even more painful to realize that I couldn't do much to change it. It was difficult to believe in the love that Jesus supposedly preached when I didn't see it practiced. All I could do at that point was vow that when I grew up I would not do as my elders, but would treat all people fairly. (I didn't know then that this train of thought was turning me into a very self-righteous young person.)

More awakenings awaited me when I moved to the city of Manila to go to college. I had decided to major in communications, thinking that some day I might be able to help the poor people in the barrios of our town. When I was in high school, I was struck by the fact that the kids from the barrios were just as smart or even smarter than us "town kids." Young people from the barrios, though, rarely went beyond high school because of their poverty and because they were unaware of opportunities that were available. For example, I got a full-tuition scholarship to attend the Ateneo de Manila University. It's run by the Jesuits and is one of the best (also meaning elite and expensive) schools in the Philippines. Without the scholarship my family could never have afforded an Ateneo education, despite my parents' steady income. I got the scholarship not because I was extraordinarily brilliant, but because I fit a profile: my parents' income was low enough and because I came from a small province, I balanced the school's geographical distribution statistics.

Most important of all, I was aware that such opportunities existed. The kids from the barrio didn't know about them. Besides, they missed school a lot of the time because they were busy working in the fields. But they usually had a radio with them, even in the fields, to keep up with the soap operas. I thought that if I majored in communications I could work with mass media, mainly radio, and give these kids a broader horizon, give them a chance.

However, the more and more exposed I was to the world of media, the roles of power and money in it, and the bulk trash it churned out, the more disillusioned I became. Even more self-righteous, I told myself I didn't want to be tainted by that world.

Meantime, at the Ateneo I was taking required courses in theology and philosophy. They opened my eyes and renewed my faith. They helped me frame my earlier questions and they motivated me to ask even more questions. I remember sitting in my first-year theology class and finally understanding what the Holy Trinity is all about, that it is God's love flowing to us, flowing through Jesus and the Holy Spirit, and that we in turn are invited to let that love overflow from us to others. This had great appeal for me. I had an image of a waterfall continually flowing. This flowing of love made so much more sense than the triangle, the ever-watching eye, or the dove of my childhood. But, most important, I felt that I finally understood God's unconditional love for every one of us, for me. I had grown up thinking that I was not really lovable; I was short, loud-mouthed, opinionated, in one word, unattractive, but I was too proud to show my insecurity. I thought my father loved me only because I got good grades. I thought I was an embarrassment to my handsome and very popular smart older brother. I know now that my insecurities were born out of the fact that praise was seldom given out in my family, affection was rarely displayed, and because I also suffered from ordinary teenage angst.

At the Ateneo, I was introduced to theology that was liberative. I became acquainted with Jesus of Nazareth, the social activist and reformer. He spoke with and asked for a drink from the Samaritan woman, he dined with tax collectors, he told Martha to stop fussing in the kitchen and pay attention, he got angry and turned the tables upside down in the temple. And he did all this in the name of justice and love, even though the norms of society forbade him to do so. This was my Jesus—real, passionate, and down to earth. He was no longer the cute child Jesus of my childhood, bedecked in glitter, or the dead, bloody Jesus of Good Friday. Finally, Jesus came alive for me.

I was also introduced to the theology of liberation through the life of Oscar Romero and the struggle of the churches in Latin America. And, yes, I learned that these struggles were present in my own country. While I was living a peaceful existence in my small town, oppression and persecution were common throughout the Philippines. While I was wondering how come we could bully our tenants and why the statue of Mary Magdalene was dressed better than the people, there were already people within the church who had noticed the same things and were working to change them, and there were also people who were being persecuted for doing so.

My faith was renewed. There was hope for the church and hope for the people. Although I wanted to follow that Jesus, I wasn't ready to make the leap. I was attracted, but still held back. I felt like the rich young man who couldn't forsake his riches when Jesus told him it was required to follow him.

Then graduation came, with its tough choices. Would I choose power-dressing, the power-steering life of "yuppies," or a life of service? I wanted to serve but I also wanted to earn enough money to give me the comforts I was used to; I didn't want to have to depend on my family.

A job at a refugee camp in the Philippines working with Vietnamese refugees seemed the perfect answer. Because I worked with an international organization, I received a good salary for my "service" work with Amerasian young adults. Most were the children of American fathers and Vietnamese mothers, usually soldiers and prostituted women. They had grown up as street children and were poor and uneducated. I was supposed to help them prepare for resettlement in another culture without giving up who they were. Knowing and appreciating their own culture was the first step, so we looked backed into their lives. As a twenty-year-old college graduate, how pompous I was to say that I was teaching them. They were as old if not older than I and they had been through life's "school of hard knocks." In the end, they taught me much more than I taught them, including the meaning of trust, as they shared their lives with me. And they challenged me to face my own story, not to run away from my feelings, and not to let my heart grow cold because of past hurts.

Working and living in the camp with people from different cultures opened my eyes to the beauty of each and how much richer we all would be if we shared our cultures with one another. Yet, as I saw Vietnamese discriminate against Amerasians, or Filipino vendors cheat refugees in the market, or how the welcome of refugees depended on the fairness of their skin and the straightness of their noses, I also realized how flawed each of our cultures is. Prior to that, I had always thought how much better off we Filipinos would have been if we had not been colonized by the Spanish and Americans. After my experience in the camp, I realized while each culture is rich and beautiful, no one culture is perfect. We need an equal exchange and understanding of each other, of each culture, to make a perfect whole.

At this time I began flirting with the idea of an alternative way of living. I speculated on how nice it would be if we lived harmoniously with each other, equally and justly, recognizing the dignity and uniqueness of each person. Wouldn't it be nice to see people—men, women, black, white, brown, short or tall, thin and fat—together? No one would be above or below, but everyone would form one big circle. We would all work together for a better, gentler world where everyone would feel they were loved and valued.

With these thoughts in mind, I chanced upon a poster of the Maryknoll Sisters inviting women to share in a "multi-cultural community engaging in cross-cultural mission, building bridges and healing a broken world." It sounded just like what I was looking for so I gave them a call. I had no idea who they were, except that they were Sisters. In the Philippines, that immediately conjures an image of discipline, habits, and stern looks. I doubted that I wanted to be one, but their poster looked appealing. So off I went to visit them. You can imagine my surprise when I was welcomed by a group of smiling, casually dressed women. On that first visit, I felt at home. Since then Maryknoll has been my home.

Why the Maryknoll Sisters? Why a vowed religious life? It's hard for me to give a precise answer. Last year when I renewed my vows, I saw my vows as my response of love to the invitation of love extended by our God, who is love. This isn't a very practical answer and, as a communications major, I know there are too many "loves" in that sentence. But that is exactly how I felt when I pronounced my vows. If there are too many "loves" in one sentence, perhaps it makes up a little for the lack of love in our world at the moment. Maybe my love will overflow.

This was my dream coming true: a dream of God's reign here on earth, a dream of a gentler world, a world where everyone feels loved and valued as they should be as children of God. Several times I thought I had to let go of this dream. I was afraid that in order to survive and thrive in this world of ours, I had no choice but to join the race to nowhere, to flow with the mainstream. But my meeting Jesus Christ in the eyes of Oscar Romero, in the eyes of countless Filipino men and women struggling to make a faithful, dignified living, in the eyes of Vietnamese refugees and Maryknollers, and now in the eyes of Cambodians allows me not only to continue dreaming but to make my dream a reality, no matter how long it takes.

And so to Cenon, I can say, "Yes, Cenon, dare to dream and never let go of your dreams."

18

Growth in Grace through Children

James and Margaret Petkiewicz

Georgetown University. For many Georgetown serves as a stepping stone to prestigious and money-making remunerative positions in the work force. For us it was the catalyst that propelled us to live and work with an eye to impacting the unjust poverty in which so many live. We were fortunate enough to participate in a post-graduation service year in Peru through a program started by a Jesuit theologian from Georgetown.

But ours is not a sob story of heart-wrenching self-sacrifice. Rather, it is a story of great privileges: the privilege of growing up in the U.S. middle class in the latter half of the twentieth century, with intact nuclear families that gifted us with unconditional love; the privilege of education; and the privilege of sharing life, and learning from those who, for want of a bank account, could be our current masters and will be our future judges rather than our indentured *maquiladora* servants.

We met during the second semester of our senior year at Georgetown as we were both preparing for a year of volunteer service near the odoriferous industrial fishing port of Chimbote, Peru. The time we spent in Peru as young, still-wet-behind-the-ears college graduates opened our eyes and our hearts to the shocking poverty in which the majority of the world's inhabitants struggle to survive on a daily basis.

We went with the idea of "giving back to our Peruvian brothers and sisters" something of the tremendous blessings we were privileged to have received in our young lives. But we received so much more than we could have ever given. Lessons of love, sharing, community, struggle, and full participation in the human family stretched us and pushed us to reconfigure our self-conceptions and rethink our life goals. Our experience in Peru forced us to ask, "Who is truly living the gospel according to Jesus?" Those whom we met and got to know lived with a faith a million times stronger than our own; their faith was contagious and shared with others willing to open their own hearts to the full spectrum of emotions in an honest, stripped-to-the-essentials human life.

Ultimately, we were forced to realize that the abundant material welfare of northern, industrial youth such as ourselves is intrinsically tied to the plight of so many unknown sisters and brothers around the world. While we purchased certain blue jeans, or shoes, or music because of the fashion demands of our peer groups, the very same people who made those items in international factories earned wages that were usually well below subsistence level. Our standard of living was made possible because of the inhumane "salaries" paid to assemblage workers and basic laborers at plants around the world.

While in Peru, we met and lived with those same people. And when we saw the faces of our sisters and brothers who suffer in such harsh and seemingly unfair conditions, it became much harder for us to deny that we played a role in the proliferation of their circumstances. The gift of exchange programs, volunteer service, and grassroots involvement also brought the pain of confronting injustice on a personal level and accepting our responsibility as global citizens.

This realization, in combination with the awesome love and inexplicable joy showered upon us by our Peruvian hosts, made us achingly aware of the need to continue our involvement in lives of service with the materially disadvantaged. As single people we both knew that this work of justice and development was what we wanted to do in the future. What a gift, then, to figure out that we loved each other and would be able to dedicate ourselves as a team to lives of striving to serve.

After one year in Peru, we returned to the United States to study and work with the homeless. We knew, though, that the contagious spark of life in Latin America still burned deep within our hearts and buoyed our souls. Five years later, we joined Maryknoll as lay missioners with our fourteen-month-old son, Shayne. We chose the lay mission program at Maryknoll because we knew of its long experience with families in mission and its focus on social justice.

Now in Oaxaca, Mexico, with Shayne, who is eight, and our Mexican-born daughter DiDi, who is five, we approach the seven-year anniversary of our departure from U.S. *terra firma*. But, in many senses, the ground under our feet has never been firm and unwavering since we opened ourselves up to learning from the suffering and daily struggles of the marginalized peoples of *Madre Tierra* (Mother Earth).

In 1995, while in Oaxaca, we endured our own share of suffering. Those of us who are white, carry a U.S. passport, have health care, and plane tickets "home" are not accustomed to lives filled with daily suffering or injustice. But we have found that when we are able to see and listen and feel with quiet hearts the songs that are sung to us and the tapestries woven for us we humbly learn the educational power of suffering.

During most of 1995 Jim was sick with a variety of parasitic and amoebic diseases. For someone who felt young, who wanted to offer his talents, and who was dedicated to "making a difference," the days and weeks passed slowly, interminably; he felt inadequate and useless traipsing from bed to bathroom and back again. This was a time when our Mexican mission life challenged our commitment to service work, our foundational beliefs in a loving God, and our primary relationships.

Life became even more difficult. Eventually, Jim had to return to Maryknoll in New York to receive proper medical care that

LINDA UNGER

Jim and Mags with their two children, Shayne and DiDi, in Oaxaca, Mexico.

would, hopefully, end his nine-month illness and allow us to remain in Oaxaca. Then Mags was involved in a car accident that took the life of five-year-old Estefani, a young girl who had unwittingly run into traffic.

We had come to Oaxaca to serve the Mexicans, trying to join in making their lives a little bit better. Now we had a very tangible sign—the death of a cute little girl—that maybe, just maybe, our best efforts and most sincere hopes and dreams might not be all that useful after all. We had believed that faith without action was a dead faith. What were we now to do with that belief in the face of such heartache and family suffering? What kind of a God did we hold in our souls that would draw us to Latin America, to mission, to Maryknoll, and then allow such an illogical tragedy? As twenty-something *gringos* what had we possibly hoped to contribute to life in the poorest of the Mexican states? How was our role as "the missioners" to be defined and acted out now? How could our presence still have a positive impact?

We needed to grow up. We needed to feel, intensely, a suffering equal to that of our neighbors. We needed to recognize God as a loving friend, a compassionate partner who would hug us and cradle our hearts and cry with us as we struggled to understand. And we needed to be forced to receive the unconditional love, support, wisdom, prayers, and friendship of so many who make up our community: Mexicans, Maryknollers, family, friends, and people who cared for us without even knowing us. What more could we do in those moments of crisis but receive, grudgingly at first and with utter humility after a while, the power of others' faith in action?

And so we muddled through together. And we did it in community. We did not give up—although there were times when we came close—because the friendship, particularly of our Oaxacan "family," would not allow us to cease and desist. Who better to teach us? Generally speaking, the poor don't have the luxury of quitting one endeavor that appears too difficult in order to opt for a new and different challenge. Either they embody a faith in something, anything really, that carries them to the next meal or the next sunrise, or they die a spiritual, and often physical, death. It was the grace present in our lives through human companionship and natural wonders that granted us the ability to embrace the cross of suffering as a redemptive gift that afforded us the chance to re-work mistakes and to continue to dream.

Five years later the wounds have healed but the scars remain; they should, because they serve as the road markers of a human story mapped out and lived fully. It seems to us now that partnership based on respect, compassion borne out by communal effort, and relationships that flower due to the mutual nourishment of shared tears and laughter lead us on the path of what is important in living out our faith commitment as Maryknoll missioners. And, more important, we believe they are the markers by which we must judge our own lives and deeds as human participants in the development of a healthier creation.

Things we used to take for granted before our experiences in Peru and Mexico (and with the homeless in the United States) now challenge our beliefs, our faith, and our actions on a daily basis. We recognize the yawning gulf between who we hope to be in the face of unjust poverty and unnecessary suffering and who we actually are. It serves as a constant reminder and catalyst to continue to work for healthy, "thinking" children and fair-trade options with our Mexican friends, neighbors, and *compadres* who have patiently taught us so much.

At present, Mags has been working with Child-to-Child, Mexico for more than five years. This international program, begun in London, is a revolutionary program that invites children to think critically about their environment and to determine ways that they themselves can improve their surroundings. The program's main focus on education in basic preventive health care trains child-health promoters.

We have seen time and again how children can be subjects of change in their communities. They open a space for discussion about their alcoholic fathers, they start recycling programs, they encourage personal and family hygiene to prevent gastrointestinal and respiratory illnesses, and they produce fruits and vegetables in their family gardens. Even more important, they are becoming leaders in their communities, learning the importance of education and teamwork, and discovering the importance of their own contributions. These children—strong and willing and working to pull themselves out of the grips of poverty—are the future of Mexico.

Jim, who has just completed a term in the leadership team of Maryknoll's lay missioners, continues to work, along with his parents, to develop T&C Imports. This initiative is a fair-trade import firm incorporated in Massachusetts that works with artisans and cooperatives around the world to provide them a fair price for their products. T&C Imports also helps create a market niche for such products in the United States and uses one hundred percent of the profits to make grants to grassroots educational groups and provide scholarships to needy worthy students.

To date, our work in this area seems to be a "win-win-win" situation. First, we are able to provide a dignified wage for talented artisans that allows them to stay in their home communities. Second, we are able to provide high quality, affordably priced items to our partners in the United States. Finally, we are able to reinvest in all the participating communities through financial support for education—whether it be a school for poor immigrants in New Jersey or a scholarship for a poor *ahijado* (godchild) who lives up the hill from us in San Javier, Oaxaca.

While this is what we adults "do," it is an almost undeniable and humbling fact that all children, including our own Shayne and DiDi, are the truest, most effective missioners. What is it about childhood—which, unfortunately, we lose when we "grow up"— that can foster such a more humane and caring environment in which to develop and evolve, teach and learn, share and enjoy? Is it children's innocence? Their natural instinct to love and to be loved in return? Or is it possibly a child's purity and inability to pass judgment? We are repeatedly struck with awe as children accept new acquaintances with a smile and laughter and share a game or a story. Their ability, maybe even their need, to be so present to the moment serves as a tangible expression of a value that could, if we were more aware, guide us tenderly and profoundly in our every decision and action.

Mission has had a wonderful influence on our spiritual journey as a family. Both the Mexican and Peruvian cultures welcome children to experience fully all aspects of life. Very little is hidden from them; children are expected to participate in the joys, the tears, the faith, the responsibilities, the births, the deaths, and the moments in between that make for a life fully lived and experienced.

These experiences are all examples of grace-filled moments in our lives as individuals and as family in which our God is alive and present. To live and to work in different cultures as missioners is a dream realized for us, a great gift of grace. How could we opt not to dedicate our lives to service to, with, and for our sisters and brothers in need?

19

Sent to Proclaim Life

Seminarian Christopher D. Schroeder

At present, I hold a unique position in Maryknoll. I'm the first member of the generation labeled "Gen X" to enter the Maryknoll Society (priests and Brothers) and when I'm ordained in June 2002, at thirty-one, I'll be its youngest permanent member.

"Young" seems to be a theme in my life. My call from God started early in life. When I was thirteen, living in Williamsburg, Virginia, I read a story in *Maryknoll* magazine about a Maryknoll missioner, a lay person, who was working in Peru as a veterinarian. I immediately showed the story and photos to Dr. Barley, a friend of mine who was a veterinarian, and I announced, "This is what I want to do." He assured me right away that I would be good at whatever I chose. I didn't think much more about going to Peru during high school, but never stopped wanting to be a veterinarian. When I finished high school, I enrolled in the "pre-vet" program at Virginia Polytechnic Institute and State University.

One Sunday a Maryknoll priest who had worked in the Philippines spoke at the university's Newman Center. After mass I spoke to him of my interest in being a missioner and was invited to go to Maryknoll for a vocation retreat. For the next four years while I was in school, I continued to visit Maryknoll for retreats and felt a desire growing in my heart as I watched videos of people work-

ing and living with the poor in other countries and witnessing to
the Good News of Jesus. They seemed to be down-to-earth people who laughed and enjoyed themselves. One of Maryknoll's
vocation directors, a priest who had worked in Brazil, came to talk
with me several times during my college years. He attended one of
my fraternity parties and even went out to the hog barns with me
while I vaccinated some pigs. While going to the hog barns was
part of my regular study for my degree in animal science, my invitation to him to join me was really a test to see if the Maryknoll
priest could party without being judgmental and if he wasn't
afraid of getting involved in the "pig-shit" of life.

When I finished college, I chose not to apply to veterinary
school. After much prayer and reflection, I decided, instead, to
pursue a life with Maryknoll. I was quite surprised when Maryknoll advised me to work a few years in my field of study first and
to take more time for discernment. In the end, it was sound
advice; I definitely needed more life experience.

I took a job as a manager of a pig farm in North Carolina that
produced 25,000 pigs each year. Although I liked my job and was
successful, something seemed to be missing in my life. Many of
my friends were surprised when I turned down a job offer that
included an annual salary of $45,000, a house, and a pickup.
Materialism and individualism really turned me off and yet, at the
same time, the job offer was a great temptation. I talked and
argued with God about what to do with my life. At that time, there
seemed to be more to success in life than an identity based on
material goods and personal achievements.

The burning in my heart to be a missioner remained constant.
It was an increasing desire to go to other lands, to share life with
people who are different from me, and to learn and discover more
about the many faces of God. I reflected on being rich in spirit and
personal relationships instead of material wealth. The more I read
the Bible, the more I saw Jesus including and welcoming all
people, especially those alienated from and on the margins of
society. As part of the baptized, I felt called to be a witness to the

reign of God by denouncing oppression and division and by announcing the power of life in reconciliation, compassion, joy, solidarity, hope, and love. That is when I entered the Maryknoll Fathers and Brothers to become a foreign missioner.

During my first years with Maryknoll, I obtained a master's of divinity degree with a concentration in world mission from the Catholic Theological Union in Chicago. Maryknoll emphasizes cross-cultural experiences for its seminarians, so I also had opportunities to work in New York City with inner-city youth from the Dominican Republic and I lived for one summer on the Chippewa-Cree Indian Reservation in Montana.

Next came my mission training. For two and a half years I lived with the Aymara Indians at an altitude of 13,000 feet in the Andes Mountains of Bolivia and Peru. Learning a new language was not easy, but I now speak Spanish fairly well. At first, it wasn't an easy life. Although I eventually got used to the cold and being without heat or hot water, the different diet posed problems for my health, and I found it difficult to get along with one of my fellow priests. Although I felt at times that I had failed completely in my first year of ministry, I had to recognize that it was a learning period— learning to trust more in God and learning to develop mutual relationships with other people. Despite these challenges, I can say with confidence that my mission experience in the Andes was one of the happiest times of my life. During my second year, everything seemed to come together as I learned to "let go and let God." My missionary vocation deepened and I made many close friends. My return to the States was quite difficult because I had been so changed by my experience in South America.

From the beginning, celibacy was a big concern for me. At first, my family and friends wanted to know how I could even think of becoming a priest, knowing I couldn't get married or have a family. However, as I learned in Peru, if I choose I can be adopted into many families. I already have godchildren and have become a part of each of their families. I also have many intimate friendships with both women and men. When friends tell me that I would

Mission training—Chris sharing the Good News in the
Andes with the Aymara.

make a great husband and father, I remind them that these same characteristics are essential for the ministerial priesthood.

Because good ministers or missioners have a great capacity for love, much like Jesus, they, like other people, may also fall in love. After five years of serving as a celibate Maryknoll missioner, I fell in love with a Peruvian woman. At first, we both tried to deny it because of my status as a seminarian. She sought advice from friends, who told her to end the relationship. Eventually, we both faced our true feelings and I was relieved that Maryknoll was very supportive, giving me time to discern between my desire for marriage or religious life. One priest told me that "our greatest poverty [as religious] is not being able to express love physically and in a permanent commitment."

After a year of discernment, I decided to continue to seek ordination. Consulting with God in prayer helped me decide that I would be happiest and could live my fullest potential as a missionary priest. While I will always treasure my friend in Peru as a true gift of God, each person must determine God's call for him or her. Unfortunately, celibacy does not become easier with time, but I pray regularly for the grace to be faithful to it and I give thanks for the privilege to live it.

Missionary life is by its very nature counter-cultural. In a world bombarded with images of measurable success through careers and money, it is hard for many people to understand why a person would give up everything to live with the poor. And success in ministry, which is all about relationships, is very hard to measure or evaluate. For me, a "Gen Xer" from the United States, the most challenging aspect of mission has been not being able to control, not being able to "make things happen," not being able to determine the outcome. In the end, though, sharing the joys, the sorrows, and the simple daily life of people enriches me. Foreign mission gives me a wealth of spiritual goods, which, for me, is more life-giving than a wealth of material goods.

As we enter mission to proclaim life and witness to the Good News of Jesus Christ and the reign of God, we focus on people's spiritual needs as well as their physical needs. Such a ministry of presence shares in all the joys and trials of life. Although, initially, I joined Maryknoll to be of service and help others, I know now how much I also receive and learn each day from others—the people I serve and my fellow missioners.

My journey as a Maryknoll priest will take me to many different cultures where I'll experience new ways in which God works in the world. Maryknoll mission teams work in thirty countries throughout the world, including Peru, Brazil, Thailand, China, Siberia, and Mozambique. Missions grow and change, as seen by new missions in Russia and Mozambique. And a missioner's creativity needs to be unlimited. In Peru, I worked with youth groups and children, with rural farming communities, and with indigenous peoples. I developed programs in lay leadership, parish ministry, pastoral care of the sick, and justice and peace. Maryknollers around the world also work with AIDS patients, Buddhist monks, and refugees.

Entering the missionary priesthood of Maryknoll has brought me a great sense of freedom. I have grown in accepting myself as a beloved child of God, even with all my faults and limitations. I realize I must love myself in order to love others and this all begins through God's merciful love for me. In my call to proclaim life, so many opportunities lie ahead. I'm interested in work in reconciliation with victims of human rights abuses, civil war reconstruction, urban and domestic violence, and also ecumenism and interreligious dialogue. God's world is a big place.

When I first entered Maryknoll, ordination seemed far, far away. Looking back, I wonder how those seven years in Chicago, Bolivia, and Peru have passed so quickly. But, then, ordination itself is a wonderful beginning, rather than an end. I'm fully confident that God will guide me in my chosen way of life as I move throughout the world to proclaim life.

*Would You Like to Learn More
about Maryknoll?*

If you feel called to a life of service similar to the young men and women in this book, or if you are just interested in learning more about the Maryknoll family, please visit us at *www.maryknoll.org.*

Thank you for reading *Why Not Be a Missioner?*